S₁ ₹²
4

PREHISTORIC INDIANS OF THE SOUTHWEST

by

H. M. WORMINGTON

Curator of Archaeology

APPENDIX: OUTSTANDING EXHIBIT-SITES, MODERN PUEBLOS. LOCAL MUSEUMS

By Erik K. Reed

Regional Archaeologist, National Park Service

THE DENVER MUSEUM OF NATURAL HISTORY
Denver, Colorado

Popular Series No. 7   Ninth Printing, 1969
First Edition, 1947

PREFACE

During the past 25,000 years the Southwest has been invaded many times. Now each year comes a fresh invasion—an invasion of those who have succumbed to its beauty and strange, inexplicable charm. There is something infectious about the magic of the Southwest. Some are immune to it, but there are others who have no resistance to the subtle virus and who must spend the rest of their lives dreaming of the incredible sweep of the desert, of great golden mesas with purple shadows, and tremendous stars appearing at dusk from a turquoise sky. Once infected there is nothing one can do but strive to return again and again.

For many, a good portion of this charm lies in the intangible presence of the "Ancient Ones", the people who lived in these enchanted deserts and plateaus through many centuries. One can see the places where they lived and often one finds bits of pottery which show the immemorial striving for beauty of some long dead craftsman. It is natural to want to know more of these prehistoric people and how they lived and it is the aim of this book to try to tell that story; not in technical terms intelligible only to the professional scientist but in a way that will make it of interest to the layman and the undergraduate student. It is also an attempt to give at least a partial answer to the two questions which inevitably arise when one considers the cultures of antiquity—"How do you know these things?" and, "How old are they?"

There is always the hope, too, that publications such as this may serve a further purpose. If more people understand some of the complexities of excavation and realize how much information may be obtained by a trained investigator, perhaps there will be less of the unscientific "pot-hunting" which leads to the looting of ancient sites and which every year is destroying an untold amount of irreplaceable data.

Constant references to source material, which are characteristic of technical publications, are impractical in a book of this nature, for they spoil the continuity of the narrative. It would be unfair, however, not to give credit to the many fine archaeologists whose work has provided this knowledge, and it is desirable for the reader to know which publications to consult if he seeks more detailed information. Numbers in fine print which appear throughout the text refer to publications, listed under corresponding numbers in the bibliography, from which the information under consideration was derived.

Although every effort has been made to avoid the use of unfamiliar terms, this has not always been possible. A glossary of technical terms will be found in the back of the book.

The task of writing this book has been made a pleasant one by the fine cooperation of archaeologists and anthropologists. It is doubtful if the members of any other profession would have given more unstintingly of their time and have been more wholeheartedly willing to help and cooperate in every possible way. I am deeply indebted to Dr. Harold S. Colton, Dr. Edward T. Hall, Jr., Dr. Emil W. Haury, Dale S. King, Dr. Erik K. Reed, Charles Steen, Dr. Walter Taylor, and Dr. Ruth Underhill for checking and criticizing the manuscript or portions of it. Their suggestions have been of the greatest possible value. They are not, however, responsible in any way for any archaeological sins of commission or omission which may follow.

I am most grateful to Earl H. Morris for graciously furnishing hitherto unpublished data on his excavation of Basketmaker houses and to Harold S. Gladwin and Emil W. Haury for permitting me to use information contained in personal letters.

The kindness of F. H. Douglas, who put his excellent library at my disposal, is greatly appreciated. Without his assistance, and that of Marian Sheets who helped to assemble the necessary references, the work could never have been completed.

My thanks are due to the American Museum of Natural History, the Arizona State Museum, Columbia University Press, Gila Pueblo, the Laboratory of Anthropology, Mesa Verde National Park, the Museum of Northern Arizona, the National Park Service, Peabody Museum of Harvard University, and the Taylor Museum for providing needed photographs. I am also very grateful to Gila Pueblo, the Laboratory of Anthropology, the Museum of Northern Arizona, and the Smithsonian Institution for permission to reproduce plates and figures from their publications.

To Mary Chilton Gray, I wish to express my appreciation of her fine execution of the cover design and the line drawings. The pattern used on the cover is derived from an encircling band on a Mesa Verde bowl. The services of Walker Van Riper, who devoted many hours to checking spelling and punctuation in the manuscript and to proof-reading, were of immeasurable assistance. I am also greatly indebted to Nedra McHenry, to Harvey C. Markman and to Margaret Roush for their assistance in proof-reading. Dr. Alfred M. Bailey and Albert C. Rogers gave valuable aid in the preparation of photographs.

Most especially I am grateful to my husband, George D. Volk, for his unfailing interest and understanding and for the preparation of the maps and the execution of the lettering on illustrations.

My sincere thanks are due to Dr. Alfred M. Bailey, Director of the Colorado Museum of Natural History, who made it possible for this book to be written and published, and to Charles H. Hanington, President of the Board of Trustees, for his constant interest in the project.

H. M. WORMINGTON

Denver, Colorado

TABLE OF CONTENTS

LIST OF ILLUSTRATIONS

PAGE

CHAPTER I

INTRODUCTION

Before beginning any discussion of the Southwest it is best to decide exactly what we mean by the word, for it means many things to many people. For the geographer it has one meaning, for the economist another, and for those who study its ancient inhabitants still another. It is in the latter sense that we shall interpret it. To the archaeologist, that is, to the scientist who studies and seeks to interpret the life and times of prehistoric man, the Southwest usually means New Mexico, Arizona, southern Utah, and the southwestern corner of Colorado. Interpreting the term in its broadest sense, he may include the remainder of Utah, southeastern Nevada, southwestern Texas, and northern Mexico. State lines and international boundaries are, of course, recent man-made devices and we must consider this region, not in terms of present political units, but on a cultural and geographic basis.

In the centuries since the Spaniards first arrived the presence of the many imposing ruins which dot the Southwest has naturally led to much speculation about their inhabitants, and the collecting of antiquities has been inevitable. The collecting instinct is such that some relationship between man and the pack rat might well be postulated if it were not that man takes without leaving anything in place of what he has removed.

From the time when the ruins of the prehistoric dwellings of the Southwest were first observed, until about 1880, there was a period of exploration and the more obvious places of archaeological interest were described and superficially investigated. From then, until approximately 1910, much sound work was done but there was an unfortunate tendency toward digging up specimens for their own sake rather than for the information which they could reveal. In the last thirty-five years or so, however, the emphasis has come to be more on the acquiring of information and less on the collection of examples of material culture. This has led to the excavation of less physically spectacular ruins, increasing cooperation with workers in related fields of science, and more careful planning of attacks on specific problems.

In a sense the development of archaeology in the Southwest may be compared with the putting together of a great jig-saw puzzle. First came the period of general examination of the pieces, then a concentration on the larger and more highly colored pieces, and finally a carefully planned approach to the puzzle as a whole with serious attempts to fill in specific blank areas. After all, archaeology as a science can justify its existence only as it serves to increase and deepen our knowledge of that strange, and to us most fascinating mammal—man.

Archaeologists in the Southwest have been particularly fortunate for a number of reasons. Perhaps most important is that climatic conditions have made possible the preservation of much material which in most climates would have disappeared in a relatively short time. Under sufficiently arid conditions the bacteria of decay cannot survive and the lack of humidity in the Southwest has insured the survival of much material which would normally be lost. Another thing for which archaeologists may be grateful is that pottery-making came to be so well developed in this area, for pottery fragments are almost indestructible. Furthermore, pottery is a most sensitive medium for reflecting change. Since it is fragile there is constant breakage which leads to the frequent manufacture of new pieces and this accelerates the rate of technical change. Archaeologists have learned to recognize certain styles which are characteristic of specific areas and periods and it is remarkable how much information ancient vessels will reveal about the people who made them.

In the course of the following discussion the reader will no doubt grow weary of the word 'pottery'. However, before he decides that the ancient Southwesterners did nothing but sit around and make pottery or that the writer is the victim of a pottery mania, it might be profitable for him to cast an observant eye about the room in which he is sitting. After the passage of five hundred or a thousand years how much would survive, if one discounted material not available in the most ancient times such as metal, glass, and plastics? High at the top of the list will be dishes, ashtrays, and vases of china or porcelain —the modern counterparts of prehistoric pottery. Also, it may readily be seen that there are differences in style between older and more recent objects. A vase purchased this year is likely to differ in many respects from one acquired even as little as twenty-five or fifty years ago.

An amazing amount of information can also be derived from the microscopic study of pottery. Trained investigators can examine thin sections under a microscope and identify the materials used in manufacture and often locate their sources. With this information it is then possible to determine whether pottery was locally made or imported. This tells us a great deal about the cultural relationships of ancient people, for trade implies contact between people which will affect other phases of their culture. In prehistoric times, when people lacked rapid means of transportation and communication, human groups were naturally isolated as they can never be again, but even then cultural units were affected by the activities of the inhabitants of other regions. Accordingly, we cannot see the ancient life of the Southwest in true perspective if we do not know something of the inter-relations of the various cultures.

One of the great boons to southwestern archaeology has been dendrochronology—a system which has made it possible to establish an absolute count of years through the pattern combinations of annual growth rings of trees. The inevitable question which arises in connection with anything prehistoric is "How old is it?", and prior to the introduction of tree-ring dating it was difficult to answer except in relative terms, for in the Southwest we are dealing with a people who left no written records. It is remarkable, however, how much had been accomplished in establishing relative chronology through the use of stratigraphic studies and the cross-checking of sites.

It is on the principle of *stratification* that most archaeological work must rest. The word means the characteristic of being in layers or strata. The usefulness of stratigraphic studies lies in the fact that in any undisturbed deposit the lowest layer or stratum will be the oldest since it was laid down first. This may be shown graphically by piling books on a table, one by one. The book at the bottom of the pile must inevitably have been put in place before the ones on top. The same principle is applied to ancient cultures. If the remains of one people are found underlying those of another, those on the bottom are older.

Rarely are the remains of many cultures found lying directly over each other in a complete series but through correlation between sites the sequence may be established. For example, if in one place we find remains of Culture A underlying those of Culture B and in another place find material from Culture B underlying that of Culture C we may postulate that C is more recent than A even though the two are not found together. In still another place C may be found to underlie D and eventually a long sequence will be established, although it may not be present in its entirety in any one place.

Objects acquired through trade are also useful in dating sites. For example, if we know the relative or absolute date at which a certain type of pottery was being made at one site, then find pieces of this ware at a site which we are trying to date we may assume at least some degree of contemporaneity.

Stratigraphic studies, of course, do not provide us with absolute dates and for those we must turn to dendrochronology or tree-ring dating.[23][121] The story of the development of this method is a strange one. It is a tale of an astronomer and archaeologists, of buried treasure that was only wood, of sun spots, and of purple chiffon velvet. Most important of all was the astronomer, for it was in his keen mind that the idea was born that was to lead to one of the most exciting scientific discoveries of our time.

The astronomer was Dr. A. E. Douglass, who was engaged in the study of the effect of sun spots on climatic conditions. The available meteorological records, of course, went back only a relatively few years and it soon became apparent that a much longer record must be obtained to be of any real value. In searching for information about climatic conditions for past centuries, Dr. Douglass thought of pines, for they may reach a great age and the presence or absence of adequate rainfall, particularly in a climate like Arizona's, will greatly affect the development of a tree. Every year a new layer of wood is added to the entire living surface of a pine. The size of these layers, which show up as rings when the tree is cut and viewed in cross-section, varies with the amount of food and moisture which the tree has obtained in the course of the year. A dry year will produce a thin ring and a wet year will produce a wide one. By cutting down old trees it was thus possible to learn what the climatic conditions had been during the years of their life. None of the pines which were still living, however, had existed for more than a few hundred years, and the giant sequoias of California which would have covered a longer span did not reflect climatic change in the same way.

Fortunately, through the study of living trees, Dr. Douglass had learned that the tree-rings over a period of years formed a distinct pattern which could be recognized when found on most conifers. Next he began to search for trees which had been cut perhaps many years before, but which contained a pattern which fitted some early portion of that tree whose cutting date was known. This led him to beams made from whole logs which have been a characteristic feature of Southwestern architecture for many centuries. By finding old beams whose outer rings formed the same pattern as the inner rings of living trees the known chronology was increased. Through correlating the patterns of progressively older trees with younger ones the pattern was finally established for the period between 1280 and 1929.

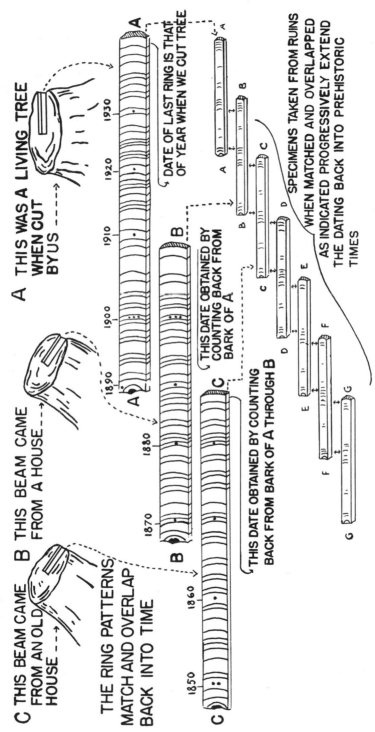

Fig. 1—Diagram to illustrate chronology-building with tree-rings. Because of space limitation the number of rings in the overlapping specimens has been arbitrarily reduced. (After Stallings.[121] Courtesy Laboratory of Anthropology.)

Next Dr. Douglass began to examine beams from prehistoric sites. From these a continuous sequence of tree-ring patterns was established for a period of 580 years. Unfortunately though, it could not be correlated with the sequence starting in 1280. Relative dates could be obtained and it could be determined how many years had intervened between the occupation of different sites but there was as yet no way of correlating these dates with the Christian calendar. The next step was to seek to bridge the gap between the floating chronology of relative dates and that which carried up to the present day and gave absolute dates.

The search for the missing sequence was begun in the Hopi villages in Arizona where one, Oraibi, has been continuously occupied since before the coming of the first white men in 1540. The fact that many of the logs had been cut with stone axes indicated a considerable age. The Hopis, as might be expected, were not overly enthusiastic about the arrival of American scientists who wanted to saw cross-sections from the beams of their buildings and bore holes in other timbers where cutting was not practical. Dr. Douglass did much to solve this problem by presenting the chief with yards and yards of beautiful purple chiffon velvet which delighted him. Dr. Douglass and his associates also did a great deal to mollify the Indians by treating their ancient customs with respect. In many cases, for example, they placed bits of turquoise in holes made in extracting cores in order to "appease the spirit of decay". One remarkable piece of timber was found which gave an extraordinarily clear series of rings from 1260 to 1344. What made it of particular interest was not only that it lengthened the known chronology but that it had been in continuous use from the time it was cut until 1906 when the section of the village in which it was found was abandoned.

Many beams were studied, but no others were found whose inner rings predated 1300. The search was next begun in ruins of villages traditionally occupied by the Hopis prior to moving to their present location. Of particular interest was the Showlow ruin, for pottery finds suggested that it had been the home of Hopis in pre-Spanish times and its proximity to a great pine forest suggested that wood must have been readily available for building purposes. It was here that one of the most famous pieces of wood in the world was found.

The decaying, partially burned, piece of wood to which the field number HH39 was given was not impressive in appearance but it was a treasure, more valuable to those who found it than any buried pirate gold for which adventurers might dig. As it was examined the climatic conditions of year after year were revealed, new ring combinations were established and the chronology was carried back to 1237 A.D., the year in which this tree had begun its life. A comparison with the ring patterns of the floating chronology showed that its 551st ring checked with that for 1251 in Beam HH39. June 22, 1929, the date on which this beam was found, is a red letter day in the history of American archaeology, for from that day it became possible to date many ruins in the Southwest, not only in a comparative sense, but in terms of the Christian calendar. Actually, of course, the floating and the absolute chronology had already overlapped but the evidence had been based on such small fragments as to be unconvincing. Duplication of ring patterns may occur if only a few rings are used. It is only if a pattern covering fifty or more rings is available that one may be assured of correct dating. It was not until the discovery of Beam HH39 that final proof was available.

In the years which have elapsed since 1929 much further work has been done by Dr. Douglass and his associates, who include many brilliant students whom he has trained. The tree ring chronology now stretches back to 11 A.D.

Great as was the importance of being able to establish absolute dates for a people who had left no written records, this was not the only contribution made by what have been aptly called "the talkative treerings".[23] The life of man, and particularly primitive man, is greatly influenced by climatic conditions and in an arid climate such as that of the Southwest the difference between drought and adequate rainfall may, quite literally, be the difference between life and death.

It is naturally an inestimable boon to the archaeologist to know the conditions under which the people he is studying lived and it enables him to understand many things, such as periods marked by expansion or by the abandonment of certain areas, which would otherwise be unintelligible.

Important as dendrochronology is, it is far from being the only outside science upon which archaeologists must depend. The records left by Spanish historians, who found the Pueblo Indians in the 16th century still untouched by European civilization and living essentially the same sort of life as their ancestors, have provided invaluable information. Also of great importance has been the work of ethnologists, scientists who analyze the culture of living primitive people. In the Southwest archaeologists are particularly fortunate, for in many cases descendents of the prehistoric people whom they study are still living in the same general area and under very similar circumstances. In spite of the outside influences to which they have been subjected there is still much to be learned from them. The knowledge of these people garnered by the historian and the ethnologist, added to that obtained by the archaeologist, gives us a far better picture of the life of prehistoric times.

Although a study of material culture tells a great deal about a people, there is much of their social, political and religious life which it cannot reveal unless supplementary information is available. There are grave dangers inherent in too great a concentration on material culture. It has been said of the archaeologist that "sometimes he cannot see the people for the walls"[125] and it is the people themselves, after all, who are important.

Two examples will show how ethnology and archaeology may complement each other. In certain prehistoric sites are found circular underground rooms with highly specialized characteristics. The objects found in these are usually non-utilitarian so that, even if no further information were available, archaeologists would consider them chambers having some religious significance. However, thanks to the fact that similar rooms or kivas, as they are called, are still in use in the modern Pueblo villages, the archaeologist may not only be sure of their ceremonial nature, but he is in a position to understand more of their significance through studying their function in modern Pueblo society. One point demonstrates very clearly how, through correlating ethnological and archaeological evidence, it is possible to understand something of the religious beliefs of people who died hundreds of years ago leaving no written records.

In prehistoric kivas are found small tubelike pits in the floors. If no other information were available the archaeologist would be forced to fall back on simply calling these holes "ceremonial". The quip that when archaeologists do not know what a thing is they designate it as ceremonial is sufficiently close to the truth to be uncomfortable. In many modern kivas, however, the same type of hole is found. It is symbolic of the mythical place of emergence or route from the underworld from which it is believed that the first people and animals came into the world. Archaeologists refer to it by the Hopi name *Sipapu*. Taking into account the conservatism and dependence on tradition of religions in all parts of the world in all times, it is not too rash to assume that the builders of the prehistoric kivas held some beliefs similar to those of their present day descendents.

Similarly, by equating what we know of the social organization of the Pueblo Indians of today with the evidence from prehistoric times we may postulate that an essentially democratic form of government existed in this section of America long before the signing of the Magna Carta and many centuries before the signers of the American Declaration of Independence were born. It may be asked, what possible information can be gained from ruins which would indicate a democratic way of life. In all the ruins which have been examined all the living quarters were essentially equal. Most anthropologists feel that had there been a marked differentiation between classes, or if all power had been lodged in the hands of a limited number of individuals this would have been reflected in the dwellings. Certain leaders and priests undoubtedly had authority, as they do among the Pueblo Indians of today, but there is no evidence of an autocracy or a ruling class.

This is, obviously, a greatly simplified explanation of some of the many techniques employed by archaeologists in seeking to reconstruct the life of ancient times. No one approach will suffice, but by utilizing many methods numerous scattered bits of information are obtained. These are studied and correlated and at length it is possible to produce an account which is at least a reasonable approximation of the **truth.**

CHAPTER II

THE MOST ANCIENT CULTURES

At least 25,000 years ago there were men in New Mexico who lived in caves and hunted animals, many of which no longer exist. Over 10,000 years ago there were already distinct groups of people in the Southwest, some of whom were primarily hunters and some of whom were largely dependent on the gathering of wild foods. Since the most ancient cultures of North America have already been covered in detail in a previous book in this series,[130] only a very brief resume will be given here.

The earliest culture of the Western Hemisphere, about which we have any information, is the *Sandia*,[64] so named because the cave whose deposits showed that it had been occupied by men about 25,000 years ago is located in the Sandia Mountains of New Mexico. In the bottom layer of this cave were found fairly large, crudely flaked stone spear points with a more or less leaflike shape and a slight basal inset on one side. With these points were found bones of prehistoric horse, bison, camel, mastodon, and mammoth, probably the debris from meals of ancient hunters who lived in the cave. Space does not permit a detailed consideration of the geological studies[9] which enable us to assign a date to this early occupation, but above the layer in which the Sandia points were found there were other layers which included one of calcium carbonate and one of yellow ochre. Geologists can interpret the climatic conditions under which such deposits were formed and they have correlated them with geologic periods when such conditions prevailed. Great humidity, such as is indicated by the Sandia Cave deposits, is characteristic of certain areas during glacial stages and the lowest level of Sandia Cave has been assigned to the period preceding the last major ice advance in the Pleistocene Period or Ice Age. This glaciation is believed to have occurred about 25,000 years ago.

The most famous of the ancient cultures is the *Folsom* whose name is derived from the town of Folsom, New Mexico, near which the first generally accepted American discovery of man-made objects associated with the bones of extinct animals was made.[25] Prior to this find, which was made in 1926, it had been believed that man had not reached the New World more than a few thousand years before the beginning of the Christian era. At the Folsom site, however, were found finely flaked projectile points in clear association with the articulated bones of a type of bison known to have been extinct for many thousands of years. These were fluted or grooved points characterized by the removal of longitudinal flakes from either face. Geological evidence from the Lindenmeier Site in Colorado, which was a camp site of the makers

Fig. 2—Map of the Southwest showing sites referred to in Chapter II.

1. Burnet Cave	6. Lindenmeier Site
2. Clovis	7. Sandia Cave
3. Cochise sites	8. San Jon
4. Folsom	9. Tabeguache Cave
5. Gypsum Cave	10. Yuma

of the grooved points, indicates that the Folsom people lived between 10,000 and 25,000 years ago.[11] This conclusion was reached by correlating the valley bottom in which the site occurs with river terraces and moraines, which in turn could be related to glacial stages. A number of important discoveries of fluted points have been made in the Southwest. Two notable sites are the one near Clovis, New Mexico, and Burnet Cave in the Guadalupe Mountains.[65]

Probably contemporaneous with the Folsom people were others who made thick, roughly flaked, square-based points with parallel sides. These points were first found near the town of San Jon, New Mexico, and are named after it.[114] From a somewhat later period we have evidence of ancient hunters who made some of the most beautifully flaked stone projectile points that have ever been created. These points, which were first found in Yuma County, Colorado, are known as *Yuma* or *Parallel Flaked Points*. They are of two types.[130] One is marked by the removal of long narrow spalls running obliquely across the blade and the other is characterized by the removal of shell-shaped spalls from either side which tends to give the point a diamond shaped cross-section.

Evidence of another early hunting culture of the Southwest was found in Gypsum Cave, Nevada.[47] Here were found lozenge-shaped projectile points, about two inches long, with small convex stems. They were associated with the remains of now extinct ground sloth and llamalike camels. The time of the first occupation of Gypsum Cave may have been several thousand years B.C. One thing which makes this find of particular interest is that, due to the protection afforded by the cave, some normally perishable material was preserved. Painted dart shafts and foreshafts were found and also a piece of basketry. Lacking direct association with Gypsum Cave type points or extinct animal remains, it is impossible to state with certainty that the basketry belonged to this ancient culture, but there is every reason to believe that it did, since it was found under a stalagmitic growth and is of a type different from that of later cultures.

While hunters roamed the plains farther north there were other people, with a different type of economy, living in what is now southeastern Arizona and southwestern New Mexico.[118] This culture, to which the name *Cochise* has been given, is believed to have begun over 10,000 years ago and to have lasted until 500 B.C. or later. The chief characteristic of the Cochise culture is the extensive use of grinding stones which suggests that the people were primarily dependent on the gathering of wild grains, nuts, roots, and similar foods. The finding of some split and burned animal bones in the sites where they lived indicates that they did hunt, but the lack of projectile points in the earliest period and their scarcity until the most recent phase provides additional evidence that the economy was based on food gathering rather than on hunting.

As may be imagined, we know comparatively little about the

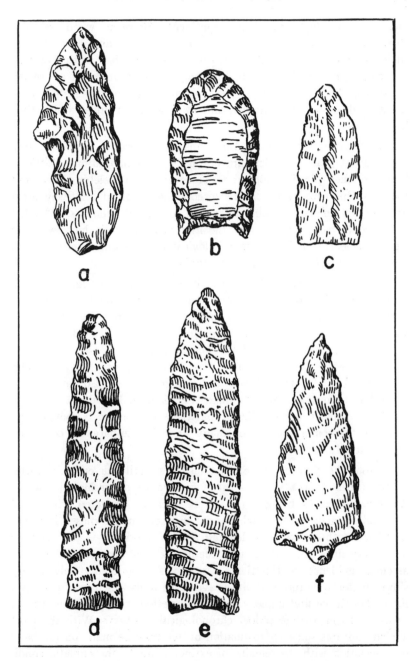

Fig. 3—Projectile points of the most ancient cultures. a. Sandia, b. Folsom, c. San Jon, d. Eden Yuma, e. Oblique Yuma, f. Gypsum Cave.

most ancient inhabitants of this continent. However, when one considers the thousands of years which have elapsed and how little of their material culture could be preserved since they had neither pottery nor metals, it is rather remarkable that we know as much as we do. At least we know something of the tools and weapons which they used, the animals which they hunted, and the conditions under which they lived.

Apparently the earliest Americans had a rather simple culture and did not practice agriculture nor have fixed habitations. Little is known of their physical appearance since only two skeletons have been found in this country which are accepted as being of relatively great antiquity by any considerable number of competent scientists.[69][70] What evidence we have suggests that the first men to enter the new world were sufficiently modern in morphological type to differ very little in appearance from many present day Indians.

The question naturally arises: Where did the aboriginal inhabitants of America come from? Man did not evolve on this continent; therefore he must have come to this hemisphere from the Old World where he had existed for many thousands of years. All evidence points to migrations from Asia and the logical route is by way of Bering Strait where the two continents are separated by only fifty-six miles of water broken by three islands. Later migrants may also have arrived from Asia following a route through the Aleutian Islands. It must be emphasized that it is not believed that there was only one immigration. Actually there must have been many and they apparently continued into relatively recent times.

From the time of the earliest cultures until the early centuries of the Christian era we have little knowledge of prehistoric life in America. Work is being done and reports are expected which will eventually clarify much which is now shrouded in darkness. It is not that the Southwest was uninhabited at this period, it is just that we know very little about it. It may readily be seen how difficult it is to assemble evidence for this time. There was undoubtedly only a very simple material culture with little save stone tools which would survive. Even though we find implements of this period, however, how are we to assign them to their proper chronological position? With the most ancient cultures some approximation of age may be made on the basis of association with the remains of extinct animals, the climatic conditions indicated by deposits containing artifacts, and other geological data. In the case of fairly recent cultures, the invaluable tree-rings

Fig. 4—Folsom diorama in the Museum at Mesa Verde National Park. (Courtesy Mesa Verde National Park.)

come to our aid and through stratigraphic studies the chronological positions of the cultures immediately preceding them can be established. For the intermediate period only stratigraphy can help us very much and stratigraphic evidence is hard to find. In the Cochise Culture, a sequence lasting until about 500 B.C. has been worked out and the report on Ventana Cave in Arizona, when it is published, will undoubtedly give us much additional information.

In the Tabeguache drainage of southwestern Colorado have been found caves containing stratified deposits, the lowest of which are believed to be quite old although considerably more recent than the really ancient cultures previously discussed.[66] [67] These deposits contained lined and unlined firepits and there were little holes, dug in the cave floor, filled with ashes and charcoal. These are thought to have been too small to have served any utilitarian purpose and it has been suggested that they may have been ceremonial in nature. Also found were grinding stones and a distinctive type of long slender projectile point with side notches to which the name *Tabeguache Point* has been applied. There was no pottery.

Obviously, a great deal of work will have to be done and probably many years will elapse before we have any clear picture of what was happening in various parts of the Southwest prior to the time to which we assign the letters A.D. If only all the descendants of the first people had stayed in the same place and placed their cultural remains neatly on top of those of their ancestors, archaeologists would find everything more simple, though probably rather dull.

CHAPTER III

THE ANASAZI CULTURE

Once we pass on to a time which is separated from our own by hundreds instead of thousands of years we are on firmer ground. Two main *basic cultures* have been differentiated by archaeologists and it now seems probable that two more may be recognized. The best known and the first to be considered is often called the Anasazi. This is a Navajo name for the "ancient ones" and is applied to the prehistoric inhabitants of the plateau area of the Southwest which includes the drainages of the San Juan, Little Colorado, Rio Grande, Upper Gila and Salt Rivers, much of Utah and some of eastern Nevada. The term *plateau* must not be interpreted as referring to a plain. Actually, it is a vast expanse of territory with a greater elevation than the surrounding areas, but with many drainage sources which have formed gorges in the tableland. It contains prairies, mountains, and terraced mesas.

The Anasazi cultural sequence is a continuous one but can be divided into successive horizons: the earlier of which are called *Basketmaker* and the later ones, *Pueblo*. The end of the Basketmaker era is placed at approximately 700 A. D. in most areas, but it is as yet impossible to give any beginning date for it. The earliest date provided by tree-rings for wood from a Basketmaker site is 217 A.D.,[122] but the culture was well established by that time. Some charred wood found in a primitive Basketmaker site near Durango, Colorado, has yielded information which is still considered tentative but which seems to indicate occupation well before the birth of Christ.[95]

The beginning date for the Pueblo era coincides with that given for the end of the Basketmaker period which preceded it. No terminal date may be given, for Pueblo Indians still live in New Mexico and Arizona.

THE BASKETMAKER PERIOD [1]

The first evidence of the Basketmaker people was discovered in 1893 when ninety bodies accompanied by a great many finely woven baskets were found in a cave in Butler Wash in southeastern Utah. It was apparent that these people were older than the builders of the cliff houses, and of a different culture, and the profusion of baskets led to the term, Basketmakers, being applied to them to differentiate them from the later people. The name soon found its way into scientific literature and has continued to be used. It soon became apparent, however, that all the Basketmakers were not of the same age, and archaeologists found that they had to have names to distinguish the different cultural periods.

Fig. 5—Map of the Southwest showing sites, towns, and areas referred to in Chapter III.

1. Ackmen	17. Keet Seel
2. Alkali Ridge	18. Kiatuthlana
3. Allantown	19. Kinishba
4. Aztec	20. La Plata River
5. Betatakin	21. Largo River
6. Butler Wash	22. Lowry Ruin
7. Canyon de Chelly	23. Mesa Verde
8. Canyon del Muerto	24. Pecos
9. Chaco Canyon	25. Piedra River
10. Durango	26. Puye
11. El Paso	27. San Juan
12. Flagstaff	28. Santa Fe
13. Gallina Creek	29. Taos
14. Governador Wash	30. Tyuonyi
15. Hopi Villages	31. Village of the Great Kivas
16. Kayenta	32. Zuñi

In 1927 the leading archaeologists of the Southwest gathered at Pecos, New Mexico, and worked out a system of terminology.[74] An early stage characterized by a nomadic life with no knowledge of agriculture had been postulated although no direct evidence had been found. This hypothetical period was named *Basketmaker I*. The early semi-agricultural, semi-hunting culture which produced fine baskets but no pottery, and for which there was evidence, was called *Basketmaker II*. To the third and final phase, when pottery was made, the term *Basketmaker III* was assigned. Clear-cut evidence for Basketmaker I has been lacking and the term is little used although the finds in the Tabeguache Caves may be attributed to this period. A simpler terminology than that proposed at the Pecos Conference has since been suggested and it will be used in this book.[110] The term *Basketmaker* is applied to the people formerly assigned to Basketmaker II and their immediate successors are called *Modified Basketmakers*.

The Basketmakers were widespread over the Southwest and remains of their culture have been found in Utah, Arizona, New Mexico, and Colorado. We know them best from the San Juan Drainage. It is probable that they really reached their highest development here, but we must also take into consideration the fact that here we have ideal conditions for the preservation of much normally perishable material, and this gives us far more information than is available for many sections of the country.

Many Basketmaker remains are found in caves along cliff faces. The term cave, although widely used, however, is perhaps misleading, for it has a connotation of darkness and of deep enclosed places. Actually the so-called Basketmaker caves are fairly shallow rock shelters, worn in the rock by the action of water and wind, and open to the sun. In them are found ash and dust deposits which contain the bodies of the ancient inhabitants and their possessions.

Many references are found to Basketmaker "mummies". It is quite true that, due to the aridity of the climate and the protection offered by the shelters, which make it difficult for the bacteria of decay to survive, many of the bodies were "mummified" with the dehydrated flesh still on the bones and the hair looking much as it did in life. These must not be confused with Egyptian mummies, however, which were preserved by artificial means and highly specialized techniques. It is simply a happy accident that these people buried their dead in places which permitted the preservation of their bodies.

Probably, though, in the Southwest as in ancient Egypt, belief in a life after death is shown by the mortuary offerings placed in the graves. With the bodies are found baskets, food, weapons, and various

Fig. 6—Basketmaker mummy. (Courtesy Peabody Museum, Harvard University.)

personal possessions. With almost every corpse is found a pair of new, unworn sandals. This would suggest that they were not a possession of the deceased but a special offering which, it is logical to assume, was designed for use in a later life.

We may now return to the Basketmaker culture as archaeologists have reconstructed it from the evidence which they have painstakingly dug out of the dust and ashes of rock shelters which had not echoed with the sound of human activity for many centuries. The problems which these ancient people faced stagger the imagination of modern man. They had no metal, no pottery, no cotton or wool, no draught animals. Really all they did have was their own ingenuity to wrest the necessities of life from a none too favorable environment. It is remarkable how, by utilizing wood, bone, stone, plant fibers, and even their own hair, they not only produced all that they needed to survive, but also provided a base from which arose the high culture which culminated in the great communal dwellings of later times.

Were we able to project ourselves back into the time of the Basketmakers and watch the people of that day we should find men and women not too different from many Indians of today. The Basketmakers were rather short. They had coarse, black hair which, while straight, had slightly more of a tendency to waviness than that of present day Indians. Their skins were brown and they had little body hair.

What clothing the Basketmakers wore, besides sandals, is not certain. Woven bands, sometimes referred to as "gee strings," have been found in a number of sites but no mummy has ever been found buried with any loin covering. Many little "aprons", consisting of waist cords to which was attached a fringe of strings of cedar or yucca fiber, have been found. Some of the longer ones, usually of cedar bast, were used as menstrual pads, but there are also a few shorter, finely woven, little aprons which probably served as skirts for women. Their scarcity, however, would suggest that they were not considered essential garments. Since the country in which these people lived is cold in the winter and can become quite chilly after nightfall even at other seasons of the year, they undoubtedly had some covering to give them warmth. Almost every body is found wrapped in a blanket made of fur and it is probable that these served as wraps and blankets for the living as well as shrouds for the dead.

The manner in which these coverings were constructed is most ingenious. Strings were made of yucca fibres, then narrow strips of rabbit fur were wrapped around them. These fur covered strings were then tied together in close parallel rows, producing a light warm blanket. Sometimes they were ornamented with borders made of cords which had been wrapped with strips of bird skins. Some mantles of tanned deerskin were also made and it may be that there were some woven

Fig. 7—Basketmaker diorama in the Museum at Mesa Verde National Park. (Courtesy Mesa Verde National Park.)

robes, for a few fragments of woven cloth have been found. These fragments bear patterns similar to those shown on the chests of individuals depicted in Basketmaker paintings on cliff faces, and they may have been parts of shirts or ponchos. It is also possible, however, that the designs shown in pictographs simply indicated body painting.[38]

The major item in the limited Basketmaker wardrobe was sandals. Anyone who has walked much in the canyon country of the Southwest can readily see how vital such equipment would be, and apparently the Basketmakers devoted much time and energy to keeping themselves shod. Sandals were woven of cord made from the fibers of yucca and

Diagram showing the method of making a fur-cloth blanket. The upper figure shows the construction of a fur strip; the lower shows the manner in which the strips were held together.

apocynum, a plant related to the milkweed. They were double-soled, were somewhat cupped at the heel, and had a square toe which was sometimes thickened, but was usually ornamented with a fringe of buckskin or shredded juniper bark. To attach them to the foot there were heel and toe loops with a cord passing between them. These cords were often made of human hair. Hair was also sometimes used to provide the secondary warps in the sandals themselves. A few pairs of large coarse sandals have been found coated with mud and it is thought that they may have served as overshoes for wear in bad weather.

Whatever the Basketmakers may have lacked in clothing, they compensated for with jewelry and ornaments. Our information is derived not only from mortuary finds but also from pictures painted on cliff faces by the Basketmakers themselves. Hair ornaments were widely used. Most of them consisted of bone points tied together to form

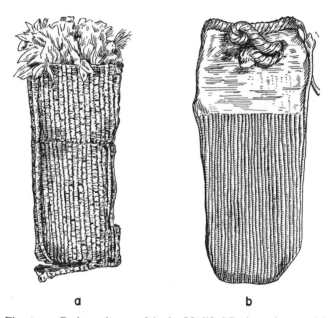

a   b

Fig. 8—a. Basketmaker sandal. b. Modified-Basketmaker sandal.

comblike objects and topped with feathers. Feathers have also been found made into little loops and worn as pendants. Beads of all sorts were among the favorite means of decoration. They were used in making necklaces and as ear pendants. Some were of stone, carefully ground and polished, some of bone, sometimes engraved. Seeds and acorn cups were also used to make necklaces. Shells were very widely used, and it is interesting to note that many of them were olivella or abalone which can have come only from the Pacific coast.

It seems unlikely that either the Basketmakers or their contemporaries along the coast were much given to transcontinental tours when their only means of transportation was their own sandal-shod feet, but the shells prove some sort of contact. Probably it was a contact by trade carried on through the peoples who inhabited the country between the two locales.

This preoccupation with ornamentation might suggest some degree of vanity, and it is probably true that Basketmaker men gave a good bit of time and thought to their personal appearance. Basketmaker women, however, seem to have been a practical lot, far more concerned with material for their weaving than with their own appearance. The hair of female mummies is hacked off to a length of two or three inches. Of course cutting with a stone knife could hardly be expected to provide a particularly glamorous hair-do, and the fact that strands of hair seem to have been cut off at different times, presumably as the need for weaving material arose, added nothing to the general effect. While Basketmaker women would hardly furnish "pin up" material according to our standards, they presumably seemed attractive to Basketmaker men which, after all, was far more to the point.

Basketmaker men usually wore their hair long and formed into three bobs tied with a string, one on either side of the head and one in the back. In some cases the hair was clipped away to form an exagerated part and tonsure, and from the hair at the top of the head was formed a queue about the thickness of a pencil, which was wound with cord for the entire length. The reason for this variation in hair dressing is not known. Perhaps the rare form with the clipping and the queue had some ceremonial significance, or was a mark of rank. Brushes made of yucca fibers have been found, which we know were used for the hair. Human hair is found clinging to them and they are a form still used by some modern Indians.

Having determined how these people looked we may now turn to the consideration of how they lived. For a great many years lack of evidence of house construction, coupled with the fact that most Basketmaker caves do not contain any great amount of ash and refuse, led to an acceptance of the belief that the Basketmakers either had no dwellings, or perhaps erected flimsy brush shelters which had since disappeared. Recent excavations near Durango, Colorado, however, have yielded evidence of well developed Basketmaker houses. Dates, tentatively assigned, fall in the early part of the fourth century. Doubtless, in other parts of the Anasazi province there were many other Basketmaker houses which have been destroyed by erosion, root, and frost action. Some of those found in the Durango area were in a cave and others on a terrace which had been made by cutting into the talus and removing the earth until a level surface large enough to accomodate the intended dwelling was produced.

"The house floors ranged in diameter from eight to thirty feet. They were saucer-shaped, formed of adobe mud not too smoothly spread over the surface of the excavation. The rim of the saucer was plastered against a series of short horizontal foot logs, laid to conform to the arc of the circle. These served as the foundation of the wall, the construction of which may be characterized as wood-and-mud masonry. Sticks and small timbers were laid around horizontally, and the interstices were crammed full of adobe to produce a strong, tough shell. The wall leaned somewhat inward as it rose to a convenient head height. Roofs were cribbed. Since the roof rested directly on the wall there was no necessity for stout vertical supporting timbers such as have been found in dwellings of the succeeding period.

"In no instance did a room boundary remain to a height sufficient to reveal the position, size, or shape of the entrance. At the approximate center of each floor was a heating pit (heating pit is used advisedly, because fire does not seem to have been maintained in the pits). Metates, varying from basin to trough shape, were a normal feature of each living surface. Interior storage devices occurred with great frequency. Some were merely slab-lined pits dug into the floor. Others were mud domes built entirely above the floor. The most common variety consisted of a combination of the two—a sub-floor, slab-lined basin surmounted by a mud dome with an opening in the top."[96]

Even before these discoveries were made it had been known that the Basketmakers had some knowledge of construction. In the caves or shelters they built cists which provided storage space for corn and which often served a secondary purpose as a final resting place for the dead. Some were lined with grass and bark and may have been used as temporary sleeping places. The cists were oval or circular pits, usually dug in the cave floor. The average diameter was between three and five feet and the average depth about two feet. There were also larger cists which reached a diameter of over eight feet and were four feet deep. Some were divided into bins by slab partitions. Cists were sometimes simply pits but in other cases they were lined with stone slabs and reinforced with adobe. Covers were usually provided. For the smaller cists they were normally only sandstone slabs. The larger cists often had more elaborate roofs of wood and plaster and some even had above-ground superstructures of poles, brush, and bark, sometimes capped by adobe.

Clothing and shelter are, of course, subordinate to man's main physical need—the need for food. In the period in which we first find evidence of the Basketmakers they were no longer solely dependant on hunting and the gathering of wild foods but had two cultivated crops, corn and squash. Where the Basketmakers gained their knowledge of agriculture is not known with certainty. Everything seems to point to the first domestication of corn far to the south in Central [126] or South America and it is believed that knowledge of corn and its cultivation spread to the north by diffusion.

Most of the corn cultivated by the Basketmakers was a tropical flint with small ears. Agricultural implements were so primitive that a modern farmer would be appalled at the thought of using them, even under the most favorable climatic conditions. They consisted simply of digging sticks of hard wood some forty-five or more inches in length. In most cases two thirds of the stick was round and the remainder was worked down to form a thin blade a few inches wide, with a rounded point and one sharp edge. Others had plain flattened points instead of blades.

The implements available, as well as climatic conditions, naturally influenced planting techniques which remained unchanged for many centuries. Probably several kernels were placed in a hill at a depth of a foot or more. This type of planting gives the seeds access to the subsurface water on which they must depend to a great extent in a climate like the Southwest's. Fields were usually in the flood plains of intermittent streams, and if there was any irrigation it was of the flood type.

Corn was undoubtedly stored for the winter and for emergency use in case of crop failures. Shelled corn found in skin bags and in baskets suggests that selected seed may have been kept for the following year's planting. Squash plants were apparently grown not only to provide food, but the fruit, when hollowed out, served as vessels. Other vegetable foods were provided by nature and included roots, bulbs, grass seeds, sun flower seeds, pinyon nuts, acorns, berries, choke cherries, and probably yucca and cactus fruit. The suggestion, that cactus fruit served as food, stems from a find which shows clearly the detective methods which archaeologists employ to gather evidence from tiny clues. No cactus fruits have been found in Basketmaker refuse, but a cactus seed was found in the decayed molar of a skull.

Meat was undoubtedly an important component of the diet and quantities of animal bones are found in all sites. Many smaller animals such as rabbits, prairie dogs, gophers, badgers, and field mice, and some birds were snared or netted. The Basketmakers developed some remarkable snares and nets. One particularly interesting net, found at White Dog Cave near Kayenta, weighed twenty-eight pounds, and contained nearly four miles of string.[38] It was two hundred and forty feet long, over three feet wide, and somewhat resembled a tennis net. It is thought that such a net was placed across the mouth of a narrow gorge or canyon and that animals were driven into it and shot or clubbed. The specimen from White Dog Cave had two sections, one nine and one six feet long, woven of a hair and apocynum mixture which gave them a darker color. It is thought that this may have been done to produce the effect of an opening toward which a frightened animal would rush. Various ingenious snares, many made of human hair, were also used.

Larger animals, including deer, mountain sheep, and mountain lion, were also hunted, and their bones and skins utilized as well as their flesh. These animals were shot with darts propelled by atlatls. An atlatl is a rather remarkable weapon which gives great propulsive force to the missile and which produces the same effect as would lengthening the arm of the individual throwing the dart. It consists of a throwing stick about two feet long, two inches wide and half an inch thick, with a prong in one end into which was fitted the hollow butt of a spear or dart. Near the middle were two loops through which the fingers of the thrower passed. The spear portion consisted of two parts, a feathered shaft five to six feet long and about half an inch in diameter with a hollow end which fitted into the prong on the atlatl and a foreshaft of hard wood, some five or six inches long, tipped with a stone point. It was set into a hole in the end of the main shaft. This foreshaft was probably used to prevent the loss of the entire spear or dart while removing it when the fore part was buried in an animal's body. Also, if a wounded animal ran away the shaft proper would shake loose from the imbedded foreshaft and fall out.

Polished stones are often found lashed to the under-sides of atlatls. It may be that they were designed to act as weights to give proper balance to the weapon, but another possibility, suggested by their unusual shapes and careful finish, is that they were charms or fetishes and served no utilitarian purpose.

Often found associated with atlatls are curved sticks two to three feet long, marked by longitudinal grooves, extending from the handle to the top and usually with one or more interruptions in the lines. These are sometimes referred to as rabbit-sticks and it was first thought

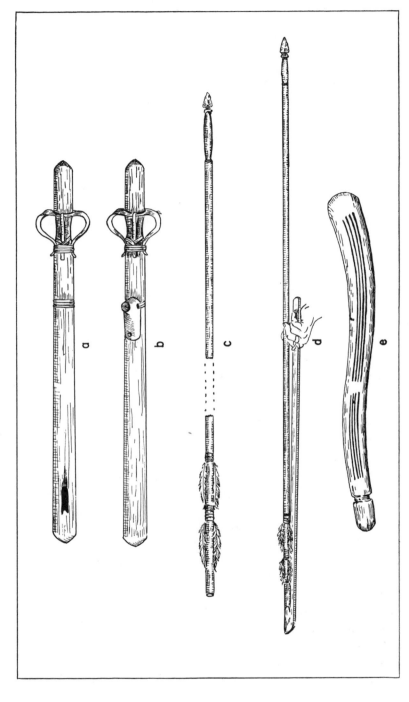

Fig. 9—a. Atlatl, b. Reverse side of atlatl showing stone, c. Dart showing shaft (mid-section removed), foreshaft, and point, d. Method of using atlatl, e. Grooved club.

that they represented a form of non-returning boomerang such as is used in hunting rabbits by the Hopi Indians. Now, however, they are believed to be "fending sticks" such as were used by the Maya for defense against the atlatl.[95] A dart or spear thrown with an atlatl moves fairly slowly and could be deflected by the skillful use of such a club. They could also serve as weapons in close fighting. There is not much evidence of violent death among the Basketmakers, but there is some and the atlatl must have been used to kill men as well as animals. Although the Basketmakers did not use the bow and arrow, they apparently were in contact with people who did. In Canyon del Muerto in Arizona evidence of a massacre of Basketmakers was found. Among the bodies which had been allowed to decay before burial was that of an old woman with an arrow foreshaft between the ribs and skin of her left side.[92]

Once the Basketmakers had acquired their food, there naturally arose the question of cooking it. Meat presented no real problem, for it could be baked or roasted without culinary vessels or could even be eaten raw. Dried corn, however, which comprised so important a part of the Basketmaker diet, was something else again. From the grinding stones found in Basketmaker sites we know that corn was ground, as it is by Indians even today. To grind corn only simple implements are needed. The dry corn is placed on a flat stone, known as a *metate*. The kernels are then pounded and rubbed with a stone, of a size which can be held easily, called a *mano*. Once the corn is made into meal it can be moistened and formed into little cakes to be baked on hot stones.

Probably, even without having any utensils which would seem suitable for cooking to us, it was possible for the Basketmakers to cook a variety of foods by boiling or stewing. To speak of boiling foods when the only available container is a basket may seem incredible but it can be done. The Basketmakers, as their name implies, made many baskets. These were remarkably fine and often so closely woven as to make suitable receptacles for liquids. Even though the baskets could hold water, however, the problem remains as to how they could be heated, since the baskets obviously could not be subjected to fire. The technique employed by other people faced with the same problem has been to drop hot stones into the liquid, replacing them with other hot stones as they cool, until the necessary temperature is achieved. Skin receptacles can also be used in the same way. In Basketmaker sites are found scooplike wooden objects, charred, and with worn edges. They are excellent digging implements and were probably used in digging cists, but the charring suggests that they may have been used in pairs to lift hot rocks from the fire and drop them into baskets or skin bags in which food was being stewed.

The most distinctive feature of the Basketmaker culture, as is implied by the name, was the making of basketry. Most baskets were made by the coiled technique in which a basket is built up from the base by a growing spiral coil. As the basket progresses, each coil is sewed to the one below with a thin splint. The coil itself consists of two rods, usually willow, and a bundle of fibrous material. In sewing the coils together a bone awl is used to pass the splint through the fiber bundle.

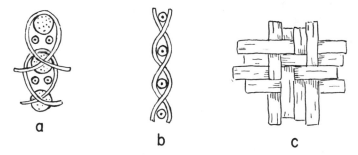

Fig. 10—Weaving techniques. a. coiling, b. twining, c. twilling.

The most common basket forms were shallow trays anywhere from three inches to three feet in diameter. Smaller baskets tended to be deeper than the larger models. There were also bowl forms, with steeply flaring sides and flat bottoms, which may have been used for cooking. Small baskets with restricted openings, which are called trinket baskets, were probably used to store seeds and small objects. Two distinctive forms are carrying and water baskets. Both are large, with flaring sides and pointed bottoms. Water baskets had smaller constricted openings, presumably to keep the water from splashing out. They were lined with pitch made of pinyon gum. Some of the other baskets are so tightly woven as to hold water, but these specialized forms were specially treated, possibly because water was kept in them for a sufficiently long time that, without the protection of the pitch, they would have become water-logged and lost their usefulness.

Both the carrying and water baskets are so shaped as to fit against the shoulders and it is believed that they were carried on the back, probably with a tump strap running from the basket over the forehead of the bearer. This type of woven strap, which is commonly found in Basketmaker sites, is a device which helps to support and keep in place a burden carried on the back while leaving the hands free. It would be particularly useful in cases where there were cliffs to be negotiated and it was essential to be able to utilize hand holes pecked in the rock faces. Some of the water baskets are nearly two feet

Fig. 11—Basketmaker coiled baskets. (Courtesy Peabody Museum, Harvard University.)

high and could have held some two or three gallons of water. Since all the water used in the caves would have to be carried up from streams below, or brought down from mesa tops where rain water had accumulated in natural basins or depressions, supplying the needs of a household would be no light chore, and the Basketmakers must have needed all the help which their tump straps provided.

Although baskets and carrying straps were utilitarian objects, their decorative possibilities were not overlooked. Many of the baskets had red and black designs formed by dyeing the sewing splints.

Another technique which was employed, primarily for the production of bags and to a limited extent in the making of baskets, was twining. In twining, splints or threads are intertwined around a foundation of radiating rods or threads. Twined bags are very characteristic of the Basketmaker culture. These are soft, seamless sacks which vary in size from a few inches to two or more feet in length. They are egg-shaped with slightly pointed bottoms and somewhat constricted necks. Usually they were made of the fiber of apocynum, but some yucca fiber was also used. Most of the bag was of the warm yellowish brown of the undyed fiber but decoration was provided by dyeing some of the

threads red or black and weaving in designs in horizontal bands. There
was no introduction of specially dyed elements. When a change in
color was desired, weft threads were simply rubbed with color. Possibly the finished article was treated in some way to fix the dye. Burden
or tump straps and narrow sashes were also twined-woven and similarly decorated.

Fig. 12—Basketmaker carrying basket, with tump strap. (Courtesy
Peabody Museum, Harvard University.)

A few examples have been found in which the designs were painted
on finished bags. These painted designs were placed on the bag interior as well as on the exterior and ingenious markers were woven into
the fabric to serve as guides for duplicating the pattern on the reverse
side.[37] The smaller bags have been empty when found. Medium sized
ones have been found containing corn meal and something resembling
dried fruit. The largest ones were often split and used for mortuary
wrappings, particularly for children. Other bags were woven of cedar

bast. They had a large mesh and could have contained only large objects.

Another type of bag represented in Basketmaker sites is made of skin. Most of these were formed from the skins of two small animals, usually prairie dogs. The animals were skinned forward from the back legs to the nose. The two skins were then sewed together with the neck of the bag formed by the two heads. They are usually found to contain

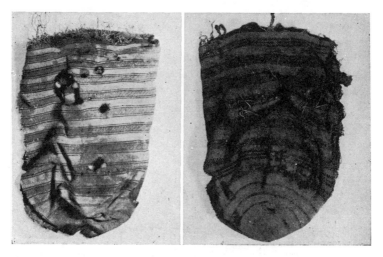

Fig. 13—Basketmaker twined-woven bags. (Courtesy Peabody Museum, Harvard University.)

oddly-shaped stones or other objects thought to have some ceremonial significance.

Although the Basketmakers did not have true pottery, they did have some sun-dried clay dishes. These usually contained a vegetable temper or binding material, such as cedar bark, to prevent cracking, and were molded in baskets. It is not known whether the idea of pottery, but not the technique for producing it through firing, had reached the Basketmakers from some other people, or if the idea of making the sun-dried dishes was one which they developed themselves. Most archaeologists believe that the whole concept of clay containers came from other people, but it is not impossible that the idea developed from the practice of putting clay in baskets while constructing cists.[93] [95] If clay were left for some time in a basket it would naturally harden and, if the center portion had been scooped out, the hardened residue in the basket would produce a vessel of sorts. Toward the close of the

Basketmaker period some vessels were made without molds, and sand began to replace vegetable fibers as a tempering material.

Most of the information we have about the Basketmakers we owe to their burial practices and to their habit of placing extensive mortuary offerings with their dead. There may have been some graves in the open, but these have not been found. Those we know are from caves. Where cave floors were covered with rocks, bodies were sometimes placed in crevices. Usually, however, they were placed in pits or cists which had originally been constructed for storage. There were many multiple burials and up to nineteen bodies have been found in a single grave, although two or three is the normal number. Usually all the bodies seem to have been buried at the same time and, since there is rarely any indication of violence, we may assume that epidemics must sometimes have occurred. It is rare that the cause of death can be determined, but in an occasional case, it is possible. The body of one young man was found with a bladder stone, large enough to have caused death, lying in his pelvic cavity.[37]

The bodies were tightly flexed, with the knees drawn up almost to the chin. This must have been done soon after death occurred and before the body had stiffened. Bodies were usually wrapped in fur blankets, but occasionally tanned deer skins were used. In some cases a large twined bag split down one side provided an inner covering. A large basket was usually inverted over the face. In addition to these and other baskets, mortuary offerings included sandals, beads and ornaments, weapons, digging sticks and other implements, and cone-shaped stone pipes. It is not known what was smoked in these pipes, but some form of wild tobacco may have been used. It is unlikely that they were smoked for pleasure. More probably the blowing of smoke had some ceremonial significance, as it does with many living Southwestern Indians who connect smoke clouds with the rain clouds which play such an important part in their lives and which are accordingly represented in their religious rites. Bodies were sometimes incased in adobe, but this was rather rare. Usually the pit was lined with bark, grass, or fiber, and the body covered with the same material.

Some quite unusual graves have been found.[37] One contained the mummy of a man wearing leather moccasins, the only ones ever found in a Basketmaker site. This individual had been cut in two at the waist and then sewed together again. Another interesting burial was that of a girl about eighteen years old and a young baby.[76] Under the shoulders of the girl's mummy was the entire head skin of an adult.

The scalp and facial skin had been removed in three pieces, dried or cured in some way, then sewed back together again. The hair was carefully dressed, and the face and tonsure part of the scalp painted with red, white, and yellow. It had apparently been suspended around the girl's neck and may have been some sort of a trophy.

There was a high mortality rate for children and infants. Their burials were handled somewhat differently from those of adults. Young children were sometimes buried in baskets, sometimes in large bags. Babies were usually buried in their cradles. These were ingeniously constructed with a stick bent to form an oval and filled with a framework of rods placed in a criss-cross arrangement and tied. The cradles were padded with juniper bark and covered with fur-cloth blankets, often made of the white belly skins of rabbits. Babies were tied in the cradle with soft fur cord. The cradle could be carried on the mother's back, hung on a branch, propped against a rock or tree, or laid on the ground. Diapers were made of soft juniper bark. Pads were used to prevent umbilical hernia. These were made of wads of corn husks or grass or a piece of bark, wrapped in a piece of prairie dog skin and tied in position with a fur cord. The umbilical cord was dried and tied to a corner of the outer blanket used in the cradle.

The only domesticated animal which the Basketmakers possessed was the dog, and two burials have been found where dogs were interred with people.[38] One large dog resembling a collie was buried with a man, and a smaller black-and-white dog which looked rather like a short haired terrier was found with a woman. Since these dogs are not related to coyotes and other doglike animals found in America, it is believed that they must have been domesticated in the Old World and accompanied their masters when they came to this hemisphere. Probably the dogs were pets, for the scarcity of their bones in refuse heaps indicates that they were not eaten. Some dog hair was used in weaving, but not to a sufficient extent to make it seem probable that dogs were kept entirely for the purpose of providing material.

The exigencies of survival cannot have left the Basketmakers too much leisure, but all of their time cannot have been taken up by work. Undoubtedly religious ceremonies occupied them to some extent. Rattles made of deer hoofs and bone were probably used to set the rhythm of ceremonial dances. These may have been worn around the waist or ankles or mounted on handles. Whistles have been found made of hollow bird bones. There is reason to believe that the Basketmakers were not unfamiliar with gambling. Gaming sticks and bones, similar to those used by modern Indians, have been found in Basketmaker sites. The sticks are of wood, about three inches long, flat on one side and convex on the other, and marked with incised lines. The gaming bones are lozenges about one inch long and roughly oval in shape.

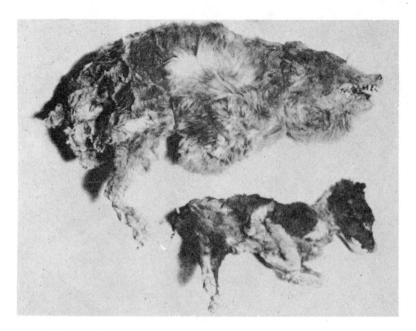

Fig. 14—Mummies of two varieties of Basketmaker dogs. (Courtesy Peabody Museum, Harvard University.)

Doubtless even in that far off time the canyons sometimes echoed with the prehistoric version of "Seven come eleven, baby needs some sandals."

On cliff faces are found pictures, sometimes incised but more usually painted, which are attributed to the Basketmakers. These usually show square-shouldered human figures or hand prints. The latter were normally made by dipping the hand in paint then placing it against the surface to be marked, but in some cases they were painted. The significance of these and later pictographs is not known, although there are innumerable theories. The most probable explanation seems to be that they had some religious significance but it is also possible that they were records, were designed to give information, or were done for amusement.

Fig. 15—Modified-Basketmaker diorama in the Museum at Mesa Verde National Park. (Courtesy Mesa Verde National Park.)

THE MODIFIED-BASKETMAKER PERIOD [1]

During the succeeding period, there was a continuation of the same basic culture, but there was great development and sufficiently important changes occurred to warrant recognition by the application of another name. The later phase is known as the *Modified-Basketmaker period* or as *Basketmaker III*. Some archaeologists believe that the cultural changes were so great that it would have been better if the term "Basketmaker" had not been applied to both periods.

The Modified Basketmaker period is marked by the beginning of a sedentary life and the establishment of regular communities. The essential continuity of the culture makes it difficult to assign specific dates to the period. A typical Basketmaker site is readily differentiated from a Modified Basketmaker site, but it is difficult to give a precise year for the time when the transition from one to the other occurred. The beginning is usually placed between 400 and 500 A. D. The earliest date yet established by tree-rings for a Modified-Basketmaker site is 475 A. D.[87] There is general agreement that, in most places, the Modified-Basketmaker period ended about 700 A. D., but some archaeologists place the terminal date as late as the ninth century for certain areas.

One difficulty in trying to establish fixed dates for cultural phases is that change and development were not equal in all areas. Dates which may be correct for the main, or nuclear, area may be entirely incorrect if applied to peripheral regions where development was slower and fewer changes were made. During Modified Basketmaker times the San Juan drainage was still the nuclear area, but the culture was quite widespread and extended north into Utah, as far west as southwestern Nevada, and south to the Little Colorado in Arizona, and beyond Zuñi in New Mexico.

The Modified Basketmakers usually lived in villages made up of irregularly grouped houses with granaries clustered about them. In some cases there were only a few dwellings, in others there were as many as a hundred. Houses were usually of the pit variety, sometimes built very close together but not contiguous. The earliest structures were circular, but later they became more oval and eventually a rectangular form prevailed. At first houses were entered through a passageway leading from the ground outside. Sometimes there was a small antechamber at the outer end of the entrance passage. The pit depth varied from three to five feet and the diameter of the structures ranged between nine and twenty-five feet. The pit walls were sometimes plastered, but more often they were lined with stone slabs. Occasionally a few rows of adobe bricks were placed over the slabs. In some cases a combination of slabs and plaster was used, in others, poles or reeds covered with mud formed the wainscoting.

The pit was covered by a conical or truncated superstructure with a hole in the center, designed to permit smoke to escape from the fireplace on the floor below. Later in the period the entrance passageways

Fig. 16—Modified-Basketmaker house after excavation.
(Courtesy Mesa Verde National Park.)

were so reduced in size as no longer to permit the passage of a human body, and entrance to the houses seems to have been through the hole or hatchway in the roof in which was placed a ladder leading to the room below. The roof surface may, in some cases, have provided extra living space since metates, manos, and pottery, have been found overlying roof timbers. Usually the basis of the superstructure was formed by four posts, imbedded in the floor, and supporting a platform of horizontal timbers. Smaller timbers or poles, set into the ground, leaned against the platform and others were laid horizontally across it. The whole was covered with mats or brush, then topped with a layer of plaster and earth reinforced with twigs, grass, and bark.

The side entrance was retained in a reduced form, apparently to provide ventilation. An upright slab, often found standing between the

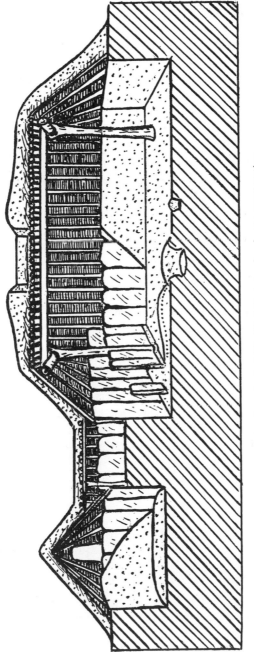

Fig. 17—Postulated method of Modified-Basketmaker house construction. (After Roberts,[106] Courtesy Smithsonian Institution.)

fire pit and the passage opening, is believed to have served the purpose of keeping the inrushing air from putting out the fire, and is known as a *deflector*. There was often a bench or shelf running around the inside of the house. This was sometimes omitted along the south side. Some storage bins were built against the walls of the house.

Floors were usually of hardened clay, but in a few cases they were paved with stone slabs. A basinlike fire pit with a raised rim lay near the center of the floor. Extending from the south side of the pit to the walls there were often ridges of mud. These were later replaced, in some areas, by partitions, sometimes several feet high, made of slabs or adobe. Metates are commonly found in the southern section, and it has been suggested that this may have been the women's part of the house. A short distance on the other side of the fire pit is a small hole, known as the Sipapu. Similarly placed holes in present day ceremonial structures of the Pueblo Indians represent the mythical place of emergence from the underworld from which the first people came to the earth. The partitioning of the Modified-Basketmaker houses may have served to segregate religious from secular activities. It is believed that originally each house had its own shrine. In later times highly specialized structures were built for ceremonial practices. This is foreshadowed in the Modified-Basketmaker period for one site belonging to this horizon has been found which contained a larger structure, similar to the houses, but apparently not used as a dwelling place.[105]

Toward the end of the period in some areas, particularly in Southwestern Colorado, some surface houses were built which presaged the type of structure found in the next period. Villages have been excavated in which separate pit houses were still used for living quarters, but there were also some dwellings which were above ground and had contiguous rooms.[83, 95]

Another important development in this period was the manufacture of true pottery. Some unfired forms were still made. Sometimes they were molded in baskets and in other cases they were started in baskets and finished by a coiling technique. To produce a vessel by this method, a thin rope of clay is formed, then wound around in a circle with each row or coil being attached to the one preceding it. Each added ring adds to the height of the vessel wall. If a smooth surface is desired, the depressions which mark the joining of the coils are obliterated. The Anasazi achieved this by scraping with a thin gourd or wooden implement, or sometimes with a piece of broken pottery. The principle of the potter's wheel was never discovered in the Southwest.

At one time it was felt that pottery making might have been a local development of the Modified Basketmakers, but this theory has been largely abandoned although it has not really been disproven. The belief most generally held is that knowledge of pottery manufacture, as well as maize, originally spread from Middle America to the Southwest by diffusion. Some archaeologists now believe that the Modified Basketmakers may have learned about pottery from people living in southwestern New Mexico who were making pottery at an earlier date.

The first Modified-Basketmaker pottery was crude and limited in form with many globular shapes somewhat reminiscent of those of gourds or baskets. Perforated side lugs were very characteristic. The dominant ware was a light to medium gray with a coarse granular paste tempered with quartz. This occasionally became black from smoke carbon. Exteriors were often marked with striations, suggesting that the vessels were rubbed with a bunch of grass while still wet. There were some bowls with interior decorations applied with black paint. The paint is believed to have been made by boiling the juice of some plant, such as bee weed, which still provides pigment for Indian potters. Brushes were probably made by chewing the end of a yucca splint until the fibers separated and were soft and flexible. Designs appear to have been taken, to a great extent, from basketry. They usually consist of bands or ribbonlike panels and the most common design elements are dots, small triangles, rakelike appendages, and crude life forms.

No kilns were used and pottery was probably fired with a conical pyre of firewood placed around the vessels. When the air is kept out and there is no excess of oxygen in the atmosphere in which pottery is fired, a white or gray colored background, such as is found in Basketmaker wares, results. Such pottery is said to have been fired in a *reducing atmosphere.* When air is allowed to circulate and there is an excess of oxygen in the atmosphere, red, brown, or yellow pottery is produced, and the vessels are characterized as having been fired in an *oxidizing atmosphere.* [15]

In a few sites there has been found a highly polished red ware, sometimes plain and occasionally with designs in black, and a pottery with red designs on a brown or buff background.[95] These wares are much better made than those previously described and this, coupled with their rarity, indicates that they were foreign to the Modified-Basketmaker culture. It has been suggested that they may have been imported from the south and that the red pottery, which owes its red color to firing in an oxidizing atmosphere, may be the product of the Mogollon people, of southwestern New Mexico and southeastern Arizona, who will be discussed in a later section. Certain Modified Basketmaker vessels were covered with a wash of red pigment which was applied after firing and which was impermanent. This is known as *fugitive red*. The theory has been advanced that this may represent an attempt on the part of the Basketmakers to produce red pottery without knowing the firing technique which was responsible for it.[7]

There are two other classes of articles made of clay, sometimes lightly fired but more often unbaked. These are human figurines and

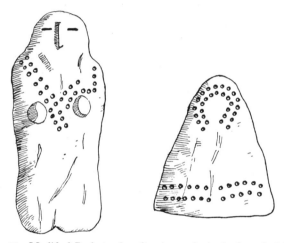

Fig. 18—Modified-Basketmaker figurine and nipple-shaped object.

nipple-shaped objects believed to be cult objects with no utilitarian purpose. The figurines almost invariably represent human females. Faces are indistinct except for the nose, which, like the breasts, is clearly marked. Arms, if shown at all, are sketchily indicated. Legs are scarcely ever shown. Necklaces and pendants are indicated by punctures and incised lines. The nipple or funnel-shaped objects are hollow cornucopias, about two inches long, decorated with punctations. They are perforated at the base, which suggests that they were once tied to something, possibly masks or clothing. There are many theories as to the significance of these traits. It has been suggested that they may have come with the introduction of maize and may be connected with fertility rites.

Pottery did not entirely supplant basketry and many fine baskets

continued to be made. There was greater use of red and black designs
than in the previous period. Sometimes these were woven in and sometimes they were painted. Sandals reached their highest level of development at this time. They were finely woven of apocynum string
over a yucca cord warp. Fringing was abandoned, and the toe was
marked by a crescent-shaped scallop. The heel was puckered. Soles
were double with designs worked in colored cord in zones on the upper
surface and raised designs on the underside produced by variations in
weave or by knotting. Carrying bands continued to be very finely woven
but twined bags degenerated.

Fur blankets were still manufactured but the use of feather cord
became progressively more common. Some blankets were made partially of fur cord and partially of feather cord. Strips of bird skin were
no longer used exclusively in the manufacture of the latter type. Small
downy feathers were employed, as well as heavier feathers from which
the stiffer part of the quill had been removed. Much turkey plumage
was utilized, and it is believed by some archaeologists that turkeys were
domesticated at this time,[87] although others do not think that domestication took place until later. There is no agreement as to whether
turkeys were kept to provide food. It is most generally believed that
they were not eaten.

At this time new varieties of corn were cultivated, which tended to
be somewhat larger than the earlier forms, and the people's diet was
changed to some extent by the introduction of beans as a food crop.
The addition of beans to the daily fare may have been quite important
for it would increase the protein content of the diet. Such a crop also
indicates a more settled life, for, while corn may be planted and then
left for long periods of time, beans require almost constant attention.

Atlatls were still the principal weapons, but late in the period the
bow and arrow came into use. This new and superior weapon may
have been brought by small groups of newcomers to the Southwest or,
perhaps, simply the idea spread to the Anasazi from neighboring people.
In any case, the bow is believed to have been introduced from some
other area. Two new implements which also appeared at this time
were grooved mauls or hammers and axes notched for hafting. Before
the introduction of axes it is believed that timbers for house construction were felled by fire.

Much of our information about these people still comes from
burials. These were more often single interments than was the case in
the preceding period. There were no definite cemeteries in the villages,

and bodies were placed wherever it was most convenient, often in refuse heaps where digging was easiest. In caves the dead were commonly laid in abandoned cists or in crevices. Baskets were still the chief mortuary offerings, but some pottery was placed with the dead, as well as a variety of other objects including ornaments, pipes, food, gaming sets, and flutes. The latter are of particular interest, for they indicate some knowledge of music. In the grave of one old man, believed to have been a priest or chief, were four finely made flutes. They could still be played when they were excavated and had a clear, rich tone. A characteristic offering, found in almost all graves, is a pair of new unworn sandals. Ornaments interred with the dead show that turquoise was now being used for beads and pendants. It was sometimes employed with shell pieces for mosaic work set in wood. In other cases it was combined with whole shells, as in one magnificent cuff, found on the wrist of an old woman, which was five inches wide and consisted of hundreds of perfectly matched olivella shells with a fine turquoise in the center.[2]

One of the most interesting of all interments was the famous "burial of the hands" in Canyon del Muerto in Arizona.[92] This find consisted of a pair of hands and forearms lying side by side, palms upward, on a bed of grass. Wrapped around the wrists were three necklaces with abalone shell pendants, one of which was as large as the hand itself. An ironical, yet strangely pathetic offering, consisted of two pairs of some of the finest sandals which have ever been found. Over the entire burial lay a basket nearly two feet in diameter. Doubtless a fascinating story lies behind this strange grave, but what it was we shall never know. Of all the theories which have been advanced the one which best explains this remarkable occurence is that the individual may have been caught under a rockfall and that only the hands and forearms could be released and given suitable burial; but of course all this is pure conjecture.

SUMMARY

In summarizing the Basketmaker horizon as a whole, we may say that the culture was fully established in the San Juan drainage in the early centuries of the Christian era, and it may have been developing for quite some time. Later it spread to include a larger area. This part of the Anasazi sequence ended, in most places, at the beginning of the eighth century.

The earliest people were dependent on both hunting and agriculture. The only propulsive weapon used was the atlatl or dart-thrower. Squash and corn were the only two crops produced. Houses had saucer-like floors of adobe, wood-and-mud masonry walls with a log foundation, and cribbed roofs. These people made beautiful baskets and sandals, produced some exceptionally fine twined-woven bags, and made blankets of fur-covered cord. Fired pottery was not manufactured but some unfired clay vessels were produced.

In the second part of the period the culture was more widespread and developed, and was modified in various ways. Several types of corn were grown, and beans were added to the list of cultivated foods. Pit houses were the usual form of dwelling, and village life began. Baskets were still widely made. Sandals reached their highest point of development, but twined-woven bags degenerated. Cord used in the making of blankets came to be more commonly wrapped with feathers. Fired pottery was manufactured, and the bow and arrow came into use. This was a most important period, for it provided the foundation for the later culture which, some centuries later, achieved a golden age that marked one of the high points of aboriginal development in North America.

THE DEVELOPMENTAL-PUEBLO PERIOD

Following the Basketmaker era comes the Pueblo horizon, the second major subdivision of the Anasazi culture. The name comes from that given to the village Indians by the Spaniards. "Pueblo" is simply the Spanish word for a community of people, but in the Southwest it has come to have a definite connotation and is used to refer to communal houses and towns and to the inhabitants, both prehistoric and modern.

The Pueblo period, like the Basketmaker, is divided into various phases. Under the classification decided on by archaeologists, meeting at the conference at Pecos in 1927, five phases were recognized. The earliest was called *Pueblo I* and was defined as "the first stage during which cranial deformation was practiced, vessel neck corrugation was introduced, and villages composed of rectangular living-rooms of true masonry were developed." The next was named *Pueblo II* and was characterized as "the stage marked by widespread geographical extension of life in small villages; corrugation, often of elaborate technique, extended over the whole surface of cooking vessels."[74]

At the present time many archaeologists group both phases under the name *Developmental Pueblo*.[110] This term, which is used in this book, seems apt, for this was a period of transition which led to the

Fig. 19—Developmental-Pueblo diorama in the Museum at Mesa Verde National Park. (Courtesy of Mesa Verde National Park.)

classic Pueblo era. In many ways the culture was still a generalized one, as was the one which preceded it, but specialization, which was to become so marked later, was already beginning. Sites belonging to this phase are found throughout the Plateau area.

Assigning dates to this period is rather complicated. It might be thought that in dealing with somewhat more recent sites, where tree-ring dates are more commonly available, it would be easy to say that a specific period began at a definite time and ended at another. Actually, such is not the case, for development was far from uniform in all places. In some sections the period which we define as Developmental Pueblo began toward the end of the seventh century; in other areas the earliest date which can be given is in the middle of the ninth century. Terminal dates are equally variable. In some regions this period had ended and the next phase of development had begun by the middle of the tenth century, and in others this change did not take place until the twelfth century. In general, the dates 700 to 1100 A. D. may be assigned to the Developmental Pueblo phase, but this represents a simplification of a very complex situation.

For many years it had been thought that the people of Basket-maker and those of Pueblo times were of entirely different physical types. The Basketmakers were considered dolichocephalic, or long-headed, and the Pueblos were believed to be brachycephalic, or broad-headed. The first appearance of the latter was thought to mark the advent of an entirely different racial group which became dominant and caused the disappearance of the earlier inhabitants of the region. It was not believed that the Basketmakers were entirely exterminated, but rather that many were assimilated and absorbed by the new group while some were killed and others driven into peripheral areas. Some archaeologists and anthropologists still hold this theory.

Recently, however, a long and detailed study of fairly large groups of crania of both people has been made.[119] The results of this investigation suggest that, while there are some differences between the two series, they are not of great significance and that, therefore, the Basketmakers and the Pueblos were basically the same people. This is confirmed by cultural evidence, for, although changes occurred, there is a strong continuity of development from Basketmaker to early Pueblo times. Possibly there was some coming in of new people, who introduced new ideas which gave impetus to the cultural development; but it is now difficult to accept the theory of a mass invasion by a racially different group and of a radical change in physical type. In the light of this new evidence some archaeologists feel that the term "Anasazi" should be dropped, and the entire culture, including the Basketmaker and Pueblo phases, should be called "Pueblo" or "Puebloan."[7]

One factor which tended to make the Pueblo people seem extremely broad-headed was the habit of deforming the skull posteriorly, a practice which became almost universal in Pueblo times. A skull markedly flattened in back inevitably appears broader than one which

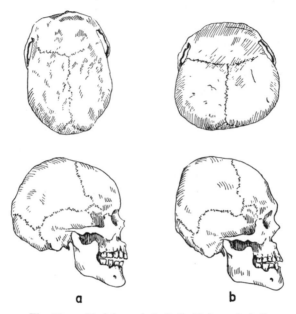

a   b

Fig. 20—a. Undeformed skull, b. Deformed skull.

is undeformed. This effect is believed to have been produced by strapping babies against hard cradle-boards or by using a hard head-rest. The soft skull of the infant was flattened by pressure in the back and, as the bones grew and hardened, this deformity became permanent.

The question naturally arises: Why did people wish to have deformed skulls? We cannot be sure of the answer, of course, but it seems possible that it represents nothing more than a matter of fashion and a change in ideals of beauty. Even in our own society there are fashions in physical appearance as well as in clothing and adornment. One need only compare the corn-fed curves of the Floradora sextette with the emaciated lines of "flappers" of the 1920's to realize that we have little eccentricities of our own which might seem incomprehensible to a prehistoric Indian.

Important changes which mark the transition between the Basketmaker era and Pueblo times occurred in the realm of architecture. There are also differences between the first half of the Developmental Pueblo period, sometimes known as "Pueblo I," and the second half which is sometimes called "Pueblo II." In a general way we can trace the evolutionary development from pit houses, with associated granaries, to the fairly complex surface domiciles and subterranean ceremonial chambers of the final phase of the period.[113] Progress did not follow the same pattern in all places, however, nor did all similar changes occur at the same time.

As was noted in the preceding section, a few surface houses were built in the Modified-Basketmaker period, but this type of architecture did not become well established until Developmental-Pueblo times. In the beginning of the period, in most areas, pit houses were still the usual form of dwelling. To the west and north of these houses, granaries were built with superstructures in the form of truncated pyramids. Sometimes stone slabs and sometimes crude masonry were used in their construction.

Later, jacal structures as well as pit houses served as dwellings. The name *jacal* is applied to a type of construction in which walls are made of poles set at short intervals and heavily plastered with adobe. At first, walls sloped inward, as they had in the superstructures of the earlier granaries from which it is believed that this type of house was derived. Later, walls were perpendicular and the jacal construction was sometimes combined with masonry. Still later, masonry was used almost exclusively. As time went by, floors became progressively less depressed. In early forms, rooms were not connected, but eventually contiguous rooms became the rule, and, in the course of time, there arose multiroomed structures, sometimes called *unit houses*. Associated with these were highly specialized subterranean structures, used for religious purposes, but apparently derived from the old domiciliary pit house.

It cannot be stressed too strongly that these are all general statements, designed solely to show evolutionary trends during this period. Actually the situation is far more complex than this would indicate. In some sections, big pueblos were built very early in the period.[7] In peripheral regions, pit houses continued to be used as dwellings long after they had ceased to serve such a purpose in the main area, and, even in the nuclear portion, the rate of progress was by no means constant, nor was it always in the same direction. For a somewhat clearer picture, it is best to consider some of the different places where excavation of Developmental-Pueblo sites has been undertaken.

At Kiatuthlana, Arizona,[107] forty miles southwest of Zuñi, pit houses and jacal structures were contemporaneous during early Pueblo times. The latter were flat-roofed, four-sided buildings, trapezoidal, rather than rectangular, in outline. Some were single rooms, and others had three or four chambers.

In the Piedra district of southwestern Colorado [106] are found jacal buildings in clusters of from three to fifteen. The different structures were often close, but did not touch. A number of clusters, laid in a crescent shape around a circular depression, comprised a village. These depressions are thought by some, to have served as reservoirs, or possibly sometimes as plazas or dance courts. Others hold the opinion, based on the results of more recent excavations in other areas, that they may contain pit houses.[41] The earliest houses were pits with sloping jacal walls. Later the floors were merely depressed, and walls were perpendicular. This type was eventually combined with two-room storage buildings of crude masonry. Next, the jacal construction disappeared and the rooms made of masonry were enlarged and became dwellings instead of storerooms.

In the nearby region of the La Plata drainage,[95] houses in the beginning of the period differed little from those of Basketmaker times, except that they were somewhat more massive and more masonry was used. There was some jacal construction, but usually a variant form was employed in which only a few widely spaced wooden supports were used. Sometimes the entire wall consisted of clay pressed into position with the hands, and the posts were absent. Stones were sometimes added to the clay, and some crude coursed masonry has been found. Stone slabs commonly formed the wainscoting. Houses were usually grouped in a crescentic form along the north and west sides of a depression containing a subterranean chamber. No dance courts or plazas have been found.

During the latter part of Developmental-Pueblo times in the La Plata area, jacal and slab construction were replaced by stone and adobe, and walls became more massive. At first the adobe was considered the important mass and only a few stones were incorporated, but, as time went by, the ratio changed and stone predominated with mud serving only as a mortar. Crescent-shaped room-placement changed to a rectangular structure.

In the Ackmen-Lowry region [82] of southwestern Colorado most early Developmental-Pueblo sites consisted of one or two above-ground rooms associated with a pit house which may have served as a domicile as well as provided a place for the celebration of ceremonies. The surface structures were of slabs topped by masonry, or were of jacal construction. Later houses were built of coursed masonry and usually contained from four to six rooms. The associated pit houses seem to have been used exclusively as ceremonial chambers. Also found in this area was a good-sized Pueblo, known as Lowry Ruin, which was occupied late in Developmental-Pueblo times as well as during the succeeding period. Thirty-five rooms have been uncovered, but there is evidence that the pueblo was modified six or seven times, and it is estimated that probably no more than fifteen or eighteen rooms were occupied at any one time.

At Alkali Ridge in southeastern Utah,[7] thirteen sites have been excavated which have yielded valuable information about architectural development. Ten of these contained Developmental-Pueblo structures. In this area, even as early as the eighth century, pueblos with as many as three hundred above-ground storage and living rooms were being built in association with large and small pit houses. These pueblos consisted of long curving rows of contiguous rooms with the larger dwelling units in front of the small chambers used for storage. A variety of wall types was used, often in combination. They include upright stone slabs, jacal, and some coursed masonry.

During the latter half of Developmental-Pueblo times in this area there were buildings made of jacal with stones imbedded in the adobe. Those found range in size from one to twelve rooms, and some may have been larger. There were also structures of coursed masonry. Some of these contained only one or two rooms but others may have been fairly large.

In excavations near Allantown, in eastern Arizona,[112] the evolution from simple masonry granaries to multi-roomed houses, and the development from simple, partially subterranean houses to highly specialized kivas, or ceremonial buildings, is clearly shown. There the change from domiciliary pit house to unit house seems to have occurred in the period between 814 and about 1014 A. D. This, however, was a slower development than in other areas. In the Chaco Canyon area of New Mexico, for example, great communal houses, with several stories and hundreds of rooms, of which the unit-type house seems to have been the forerunner, apparently were started by 1014.

Unit houses, which were commonly built in the second part of Developmental-Pueblo times and in the following period, were above-ground structures built of stone and adobe. They were one story in height and usually contained from six to fourteen rooms. These rooms were sometimes placed in a long row, sometimes in a double tier, and, in other cases, were arranged in the shape of an "L" or rectangular "U".

Unit houses are occasionally referred to as *clan houses,* for some archaeologists believe that they may have been occupied by single family groups. Present day social organization in the western pueblos is based on clans, and it is believed that this is of long standing and probably extends far back into prehistoric times. Descent is traced in these pueblos in the maternal line. In such villages a clan is a group made up of individuals descended from the same female ancestor. Houses belong to the women, and a family group which lives together usually consists of a woman and her daughters and their families. The husbands belong to other clans. They live with their wives' groups, but their religious affiliations are with their own clans. The kivas, or ceremonial chambers, belong to the men of the clan and serve as club rooms as well as providing a place where secret religious rites may be performed.

In Developmental-Pueblo times, kivas were very similar in form to those used at the present time in the eastern pueblos. They were circular, subterranean structures which lay to the south or southeast of houses. Walls were of masonry, and there were encircling benches in which pilasters were often incorporated. Roofs were normally cribbed, and entrance was usually through the smoke-hole in the center; although, in some unit-type sites in southwestern Colorado, stone towers are found containing manholes which led into tunnels connecting with kivas.[83]

It is interesting to note the apparent derivation of kivas from the old domiciliary pit houses which had, at least in a rudimentary form, all of the features of the later religious structures and which also lay in the same position in relation to the surface masonry structures. It is believed that originally each house had its own shrine. When special structures came to be built exclusively for the performance of religious rites, the people clung to the old form of building, although their dwellings were developing in a different direction. There is an innate conservatism and traditionalism in religion which is well represented in architecture. In our own cities, where we erect medieval cathedrals and sky scrapers, we can see a lag of from four to seven centuries between religious and secular architecture.

In some parts of the Southwest, kivas were not the only places available for the performance of religious rites. At Allantown [112] was found a great circular area, paved with adobe and enclosed on three sides by upright stone slabs, which is believed to have been a dance court. On the north side is a platform or dais. Probably in that long

Fig. 21—Interior view of a kiva showing distinctive features. Note the
ventilator, deflector, fire-pit, sipapu, bench, and pilasters.

ago time there were many days and nights when moving feet beat out the intricate rhythms of the dance against the hard packed adobe, as the gods were importuned to bring life-giving rain for the crops.

In addition to the houses, kivas, and dance courts, there were also brush shelters with firepits, ovens and storage places. These probably provided outdoor cooking facilities during the summer.

In the field of pottery, important changes were taking place, and specialization was increasing all through the Anasazi area. Developmental-Pueblo pottery had a finer paste and was better made than that of Modified-Basketmaker times. Some tempering was done with pulverized potsherds. More different types were represented. Plain gray ware was still made. Pottery with black designs on a white background was very common, except in the Alkali Ridge[7] area of southeastern Utah where early Developmental-Pueblo painted pottery had a pinkish-orange ground color with designs in red paint. In referring to painted pottery it is customary to mention first the color of the design and then the color of the background, as, for example, *black-on-white* or *red-on-orange* ware. Minor types of Developmental-Pueblo times included a lustrous black-on-red ware and bowls with more or less polished black interiors and brownish or reddish exteriors. The differentiation between culinary and non-culinary pottery became more marked. The former came to be characterized by corrugations in the clay, and the latter chiefly by painted designs.

Fig. 22—Corrugated Pottery. (Courtesy National Park Service.)

Specialization in particular areas is best shown in the black-on-white wares. There are two main groups—an eastern one which centered around the Chaco Canyon area of New Mexico, and a western one which centered around the Kayenta region of Arizona.[110] Both extended far beyond these nuclear areas. The former was characterized by a wide use of mineral paint. Designs stand out from the background. Possibly they were applied after the vessel had been polished. In the western form, designs were usually applied with a paint made from plant juices and they seem to fade into the surface of the vessel. This may be due in part to the application of paint before the polishing of the vessel had been completed.

In all sections there was a greater variety of forms and designs than in the preceding period. Designs were no longer confined to the

Fig. 23—Black-on-white pottery. Developmental-Pueblo period.

interiors of bowls and ladles but were placed on all kinds of vessels. Basketry patterns were still used, but others were taken from textiles, and still others seem to have been developed only for the medium of pottery. Designs show a certain lack of skill in execution, but they were elaborate and boldly conceived. There is every evidence of people still experimenting with a new medium. The principal elements were parallel lines, sometimes straight and in other cases stepped or wavy; zig-zags, triangles, checkerboards, and interlocking frets. Both curvilinear and rectilinear designs were used. In the latter part of the period parallel lines were scarce, and elements became broader and heavier.

Techniques of production and finishing differed from those of Modified-Basketmaker times. The practice of using slips developed.

A slip is a coating of very fine, almost liquid, clay which is smeared on a finished vessel before firing to give a smooth even finish. In the second part of the period, spiral coiling began. In the earlier forms, short clay fillets, which made only one turn around the vessel, were used. With the spiral technique, longer rolls of clay were used and each made several circuits around the vessel. During the first half of the period, vessels were either entirely smoothed or, in the case of many culinary vessels, the bottom was smoothed while the neck portion was characterized by flat, relatively broad, concentric clay bands.

Fig. 24—Neck-banded vessel. Developmental-Pueblo Period.
(Courtesy National Park Service.)

These neck-banded jars are quite characteristic of early Developmental Pueblo. During the second part of the period corrugated ware appeared. This is pottery in which the alternate ridges and depressions resulting from a coiling and pinching technique of manufacture have not been obliterated. Sometimes the corrugations were embellished by indentations produced by pinching the clay between the fingers or by incising them with the fingernail or some small implement. In this way simple patterns were formed. The use of this type of pottery for cooking may stem from the fact that this is the only type of decoration which would not soon be obliterated by soot. Objects made of clay also included tubular pipes or cloud-blowers. Stone and wood were also sometimes used in making these objects.

Baskets continued to be made, although pottery vessels were used for many purposes for which baskets had formerly been employed. The number of baskets made undoubtedly diminished, and the large flat trays so characteristic of Basketmaker times seem to have almost entirely disappeared. The great decrease in number of baskets made, however, may be more apparent than real, for most Developmental-Pueblo sites are in the open and little perishable material remains.

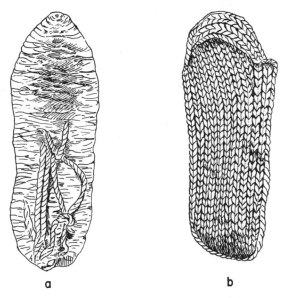

a   b

Fig. 25—a. Developmental-Pueblo sandal,
b. Great-Pueblo sandal.

Examples which have been found indicate that the coiling technique continued and designs became more elaborate. Twilled baskets were also manufactured.

Sandals of fine string, with coarse patterns on the under side, were still being woven. They had rounded toes. A new material and new techniques in weaving appeared with the introduction of cotton at this time. Cotton was grown and used to produce thread which was woven into fabrics with looms. Fur and feather blankets, primarily the latter, were still being made, but light cotton blankets were probably also worn. It is thought that kilts and breech cloths were made of the same material. Various ornaments, including beads, pendants, and bracelets, were worn. The former were largely of colored shales, turquoise, and alabaster. Some bracelets were of glycymeris, a shell which must have been imported from the Gulf of California.

Cotton was the only addition to the list of cultivated plants, but squash and beans continued to be grown. Corn was still the staple food. It was ground on scoop-shaped trough metates. In one case three graded manos, of varying degrees of roughness, were found with one metate. This foreshadowed the later Pueblo practice of having mealing bins with series of metates ranging in texture from relatively coarse to very fine. Corn was first coarsely ground on the roughest metate, or with the roughest mano, and then worked over with progressively smoother stones until a very fine meal resulted. Crudely flaked hoes began to be used in cultivating the crops. Some were hafted, but many were not.

Meat continued to be included in the diet. Bear, elk, buffalo, wolf, mountain sheep, deer, and rabbits were among the animals hunted. The bow and arrow were almost universally used. Arrowheads were well flaked, usually long and narrow, with long, sharp barbs. Late in the period a new type appeared which became increasingly numerous later. These points were short, broad, and notched at right angles.

Dogs and turkeys were the only domesticated animals. One reason for the belief that they were not kept to provide food is that they have been found buried with mortuary offerings. Corn was provided for the turkeys and bones for the dogs which were buried. There was also pottery, sometimes miniature vessels, sometimes sherds rubbed down to form shallow vessels.

Axes are relatively scarce, but are found in this period. Edges were smoothed by grinding. On the whole these were not very efficient cutting implements, for the edges were quite dull.

Human burials varied widely according to locality. For the most part they are found in refuse heaps. These characteristic mounds, as the name indicates, were formed of the refuse thrown away by the inhabitants of a village and are composed of ashes, dirt, broken pottery, and general debris. There was no disrespect for the dead in burying them in such a place; it was simply that, with the primitive implements available, it was desirable to make interments where digging was easiest. The difficulties of excavation also led to the placing of bodies, in some cases, in abandoned storage pits or houses. Children are often found buried under floors near firepits, possibly because mothers felt that the dependence of an infant extended to the soul and they wished to keep it near.

Bodies were inhumed in a more or less flexed position. There was no fixed orientation, as there was in later periods. Undoubtedly there were some mortuary offerings of a perishable nature, but these have not survived. Pottery was placed in graves in many cases. At Kiatuthlana[107] there was a strong degree of consistency in the offerings. Each grave contained a culinary jar covered by a bowl with a blackened interior, and a black-on-white bowl. Certain graves contained more than three pieces of pottery, but they were in multiples of three, with an equal number of each type.

There are some very puzzling features about the disposal of the dead in Developmental-Pueblo times. In most of the San Juan area and in the Kiatuthlana region the number of graves found is about what would be expected on the basis of the population indicated by habitations. In other places, however, and particularly in the La Plata region,[95] only a very few burials have been found and they undoubtedly represent only a fraction of the deaths which must have occurred. What happened to the remaining bodies is a question which has not been answered. Some particularly baffling finds are: skulls buried without bodies, and bodies buried without heads. In the case of skull burials it has been suggested that warriors may have been killed some distance from home. Bringing the entire body back would have been impracticable, and only the heads were returned to be given suitable burial among the kinsmen of the dead individual. This, however, does not explain the headless skeletons which are also found, for it seems unlikely that the body of an enemy which had been left behind, after the head had been removed, would be given burial.

At Alkali Ridge[7] there was the usual baffling scarcity of burials in early Developmental-Pueblo times, and no evidence of cremation. A number of burials were found in the later horizon, however, and they provide an interesting example of how much we can learn of how people lived from a study of their physical remains. Evidence of various bone diseases indicates that the Alkali Ridge people suffered from malnutrition and vitamin deficiencies. The fact that one individual, so badly crippled that she could not have been a productive member of the community, lived to be sixty years old or more, tells us that these people were willing to care for handicapped members of their group. The communities must have been subject to hostile attack. Two individuals appear to have died from blows on the head. One of these men had also been shot by an arrow, and scratches on his head indicate that he had been scalped. Evidence of local inbreeding is provided by the finding of three people with fused ribs, a very rare abnormality not likely to appear so frequently except in a highly inbred group.

Peripheral Areas

Outside of the central area of the Anasazi region there were other developments during this period. In marginal areas, certain phenomena are almost invariably present. There will be some lag in the diffusion of new traits, and in some ways the culture of the marginal section will be less advanced. Early elements may survive for a long time. Traits which are chronologically distinct in the main area may arrive together in the outlying sections. Other features may not spread or may be rejected by the people of the peripheral area. In general, there is a progressive fading of the basic pattern as one goes farther away from the nucleus. Certain traits may have been acquired from other cultures, and there is usually also a tendency to develop new traits and to modify and adapt those which have been imported, in accordance with local needs.

All of these characteristics are to be found in the region north and northwest of the Colorado River which is known as the *Northern Periphery* of the Southwest. During Developmental-Pueblo times a number of early traits persisted in the Northern Periphery after they had disappeared in the San Juan country. People continued to live in earth-covered pit houses and lodges after these had been replaced by surface masonry structures farther south. In some cases the side passage still served as an entrance instead of being reduced in size for use as a ventilator. Slab cists, identical with Basketmaker structures, were quite common. In the south and east of the periphery some unit houses were built during late Developmental-Pueblo times, but they were far inferior to those of the main district. Much crude, gray pottery was produced, and fugitive-red paint was widely used. Clay figurines and nipple-shaped objects, characteristic of the Basketmaker culture, continued to be widely made in the north long after they had disappeared in the nuclear area. Gaming bones are among the most common artifacts. Throughout, there is an amalgamation of traits which were separate elsewhere. In some cases early pottery types are found associated with houses of a later type; in others it is the pottery which is more advanced than the houses.

Certain features characteristic of the main Pueblo culture either did not reach the Northern Periphery, or were not accepted by the inhabitants. North of the San Juan drainage, sandals and cotton cloth were not produced. The turkey was not domesticated. There were no grooved axes and mauls. True kivas have not been found, although there are some structures which are believed to have been used for ceremonial purposes.

Other features, which are characteristic of the Northern Periphery, are not found farther south. Many of these are clearly shown in sites found in the drainage of the Fremont River of Utah.[97] Here leather moccasins replaced sandals. These were made of mountain sheep hide with the hair left on. The portion of the hide containing the dewclaws of the sheep was attached to the sole in such a way that the dewclaws served as hobnails. Clay figurines, most of which depicted human females, were quite elaborate. Also characteristic of the culture, were remarkably fine rock paintings and pecked drawings of Katchinas or supernatural beings. In the field of pottery, traits which characterize northern peripheral wares include raised or appliquéd ornaments and punched designs. Another distinguishing feature is a unique form of grinding stone, sometimes called the *Utah-type* metate. This is a shovel-shaped stone with a deep trough and a platform at one end containing a secondary depression.

Although the culture of the Northern Periphery is basically Southwestern in character and is largely of Modified-Basketmaker and early Developmental-Pueblo origin, it seems probable that the Anasazi was not the only influence and that there was some immigration and diffusion of ideas from the east and the north. People living farther to the north may also have affected the life of the inhabitants of the Periphery in other ways. At approximately the end of Developmental-Pueblo times, most of the marginal area was abandoned. Some archaeologists think that this was due to pressure from northern nomadic tribes. Only along the Colorado River, did northerly sites continue to be occupied during the following period.

Anasazi traits also penetrated to other peripheral areas. Evidence of Anasazi influence is found in southwestern Texas sites, particularly those of the Big Bend area, occupied after about 900 A.D. Modified Basketmaker and Pueblo traits are also found in sites in the valleys of the Muddy and Virgin rivers in southeastern Nevada. In the Nevada sites[46] both pit dwellings and above-ground houses with many rooms have been found. Most of the painted pottery is black-on-gray but

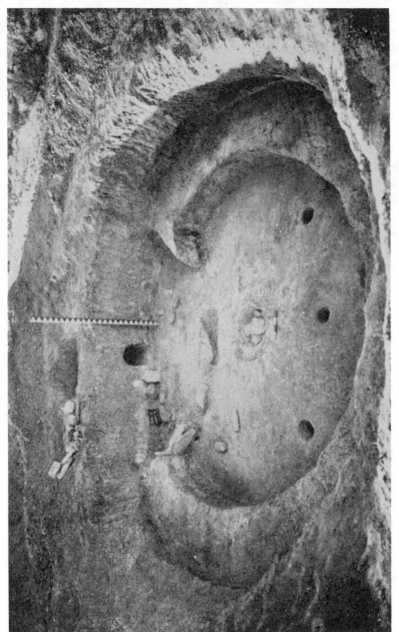

Fig. 26—Rosa pit house after excavation. (Courtesy Columbia University Press.)

some black-on-white and black-on-red wares also occur. Culinary ware was corrugated. As in Utah, there were no axes, and the turkey does not appear to have been domesticated.

One of the most interesting marginal manifestations is known as the *Rosa Phase*.[41] Rosa sites have been found in the drainage of the Governador Wash which lies between the towns of Aztec and Dulce in north-central New Mexico. Between about 700 and 900 A.D. this region was occupied by people who lived in very large pit houses. They were also familiar with surface construction and had above-ground granaries, made of adobe, which sometimes contained several contiguous rooms. Houses and granaries were surrounded by stockades made of posts interlaced with brush. Pottery was not very well made, and consisted to a great extent of undecorated ware. Many of the vessels were started in baskets. The small amount of decorated pottery which was produced seems to represent imitations of other already developed types.

The bones of a great many dogs and turkeys are found in the rubbish heaps and it is thought that they may have been an important element in the diet of the people. Dogs, however, probably had some significance other than as a source of food, for some were so old and toothless that they may have died of old age. Also, dogs were found buried in every grave.

Burial customs differed from those of other areas. In some cases, bodies seem to have been exposed and allowed to decompose, at least partially, before the bones were buried. There was no deformation of the skull in any of burials uncovered.

SUMMARY

Returning to the subject of the Developmental-Pueblo period in the nuclear portion of the Anasazi region, we may summarize by saying that this was a time of transition. Pit houses were first used as dwellings, and then, becoming more highly specialized, were used as ceremonial structures. Surface granaries gave rise to above-ground houses. Walls were first predominantly of poles and adobe, later of masonry. Large structures with numerous contiguous rooms became increasingly common. Pottery improved in quality and an increasing number of wares were represented, including corrugated cooking ware. Axes and hoes were added to the assemblage of implements. Cotton began to be grown, and fabrics were produced by loom weaving. These statements, however, only indicate general trends, for there was no

real uniformity of cultural development. There were differences between various sections of the country, and there were also variations
within the same area. With the end of Developmental-Pueblo times,
however, all of the basic Pueblo traits were established, and the stage
was set for the flowering of the high culture of the next period which
has been called the "Golden Age" of the Anasazi.

THE GREAT-PUEBLO PERIOD

The phase which followed Developmental-Pueblo times is the one
best known to the general public, for it was during this time that there
were built the great communal houses, whose impressive ruins in our
National Monuments and Parks draw thousands of fascinated visitors
every year. This is the period of the Cliff Dwellers who built the
remarkable structures of Mesa Verde and then, apparently, disappeared
into the mists of time. Much of the mystery which surrounds these
people in the public mind is unnecessary, but there is still enough of
the remarkable in their achievements, and in their disappearance from
their old haunts, to intrigue the imagination.

This period is also known as *Classic Pueblo* or *Pueblo III,* but is
now aptly called the *Great-Pueblo* [110] period, for it marks the time when
this culture reached the pinnacle of its development. Its general characteristics were summarized in the Pecos classification which defined
Pueblo III as: "the stage of large communities, great development of
the arts, and growth of intensive local specialization."[74]

There is some disagreement as to the date which should be assigned to the beginning of Great-Pueblo times, for cultural development was not equal in all sections of the Plateau. In some areas,
people were still living as they had in Developmental-Pueblo times,
while, in others, Great-Pueblo traits were well established. Since
specialization became so marked that various cultural centers must
be considered separately, it is best, in most cases, to give dates for
this period in terms of specific areas. There is, however, some agreement as to the ending date. In general it may be said that Great-Pueblo
times began, in most places, about 1050 A.D. and lasted until the
end of the thirteenth century, when the whole northern portion of the
Plateau was abandoned.

The greatest change from the preceding period was in the realm
of architecture. There were a great many unit houses, in which a
fairly large percentage of the population lived, but big "apartment
houses," up to five stories in height and containing hundreds of rooms,

Fig. 27—Great-Pueblo diorama in the Museum at Mesa Verde National Park showing Spruce Tree House. (Courtesy Mesa Verde National Park.)

were also built. This change naturally affected not only the living conditions of the people, but influenced their whole life, for people living together in a closely-knit community will develop differently from the way they would in widely scattered settlements.

When a population is broken up into small independent units and scattered over a wide area, there is not likely to be any need or desire for overall government, and authority is usually vested in the person of the head of the family or clan. As the size of the group increases and life becomes increasingly complex, some centralization of power is inevitable. Cooperation between individuals and groups of individuals becomes not only desirable but essential. In such an undertaking as the building of a huge structure, containing hundreds of rooms, there must be cooperation. With the occupation of such a building, when as many as a thousand people may be living under one roof, the need for working together continued. With greater cooperation, leisure is likely to increase, although sometimes this greater freedom is limited to a ruling caste which makes great demands on the time of other individuals. This does not appear to have been the case among the ancient Pueblo people as they seem to have had an essentially democratic form of government.

With added leisure, there is usually increasing development in the arts and in religion. As more time can be devoted to religious practices, ceremonies tend to become more elaborate and more formalized. Often a priestly caste will arise which, as in the case of the concentration of secular power, may result in autocracy. The Pueblos seem to have avoided this danger too. The many kivas suggest that religion and its ceremonial expression must have played a strong part in their daily lives, as it does today. Undoubtedly there were priests who were figures of importance in the community, but there is no evidence that they wielded an autocratic power which gave them great material advantages over other members of the group.

Community living will have other far-reaching influences. When only a small family group is living together, it must be almost entirely self-sufficient and must produce practically everything which it uses. As the group increases in size, specialization also tends to increase. For example, a woman who makes exceptional baskets, but is not a particularly skillful potter, may come to specialize in the making of baskets which she can exchange for pottery made by someone who produces a finer ware. Familiarity with the work of others will also stimulate development, for new ideas will have a wider distribution and competition will serve as a stimulating factor.

There was no basic change in type of structure, for the great houses were, in a sense, much enlarged and modified unit houses. The great change lay in the joining together of great numbers of people. It must not be thought, however, that all of the people lived in huge communal dwellings such as those of Mesa Verde or Chaco Canyon. Actually many groups continued to live in unit houses at a considerable distance from the main centers, and many of the so-called great houses contained only a small number of rooms. The really big houses were in the minority and would appear to have been capable of sheltering only a small fraction of the total population.

There was undoubtedly a general trend toward a coalescence of the population, however, and it is interesting to speculate on the reason for this tendency. The fact that the great houses were admirably suited to defense has given rise to the theory that the people began to move together for protection against an outside enemy. There can be no doubt that the need for defense was taken into consideration in the building of the big structures, but this cannot be the whole answer. There is some evidence of violence, but not a great deal. The utmost care was taken in the construction of the great houses, and much time-consuming work went into decoration. When danger threatens, speed becomes the primary consideration, and the amenities of life are sacrificed. There were many small houses in which a good portion of the population lived, and these were not always in locations suitable for defense. Since defense obviously was a consideration in the minds of the builders of the great houses, and since there is some evidence of violence and bloodshed, we cannot discount the role which warfare may have played in architectural development, but it seems certain that this was not the only factor which influenced this development.

Another interesting theory has been proposed.[81] It is based on the fact that, not only was there great building activity during this period, but also that there was much restlessness and moving about. Walls were torn down and rebuilt, and many buildings were abandoned and new ones erected, without any reason that is apparent from archaeological evidence. It has been suggested that this restlessness and the intensity with which building activities were pursued may have been an outlet for the repressions and inhibitions of a group which had a cultural pattern with set rules against violence and excess. There is great variation among the different groups which make up the Pueblo Indians of today, but, in many cases, they have a cultural pattern that upholds the golden mean and discourages all extremes.[4] Such a way of life might well produce certain repressions which would result in a general restlessness and desire for change and activity.

The chief objection to this theory lies in the defensive character of the great houses, which would suggest that violence was not unknown. In times of war, desire for change and action is readily satisfied, and socially approved reasons are provided for breaking away from many of the established rules of society. Undoubtedly, though, the urge which resulted in the creation of great community dwellings which were in essence city-states, came to some extent from within the people themselves and was not entirely the result of outside influences. Many factors undoubtedly played a part, but the building of the big houses must, in some measure, be regarded as an architectural vogue which, to a great extent, stemmed from the desires as well as the needs of the people.

The causes which led to the abandonment of the great houses and which resulted in the end of this phase of Pueblo development are just as difficult to understanding as are those which led to their being constructed in the first place. By 1300 A.D., the entire northern section of the Plateau had been deserted. This was not the result of a single mass migration, but rather of a wide general movement. First one big center and then another was deserted. Even in these centers themselves, all the inhabitants did not leave at the same time; rather it seems that small groups drifted away, a few at a time. Eventually, though, the entire northern frontier was deserted, and no living person who had contributed to the growth and flowering of the culture remained. Naturally, this strange departure has given rise to much conjecture. It would be pleasant to be able to say that such and such a cause produced this result. Unfortunately, anything connected with the human race is rarely quite so simple.

The invaluable tree-rings have not only provided us with dates for various events, but have given us information about climatic conditions which undoubtedly had a tremendous effect on the movements of the people with whom we are concerned. From tree-ring records we know that during the centuries when the hopes and fears of the prehistoric Pueblo Indians were centered on their crops there were bad years as well as good ones. We know of periods when rainfall was below normal, and of others when there were real droughts. Most of these were of short duration, however, until the disastrous period between 1276 and 1299 when there was practically no rain, and the Southwest suffered an extremely severe drought. It was during this period that the northern frontier was finally abandoned, and the people moved to new localities. Some archaeologists have felt that the disappearance of the Pueblos from their old homes can be traced entirely to this disastrous drought. If all the communities had been abandoned at the same time, this would be a logical assumption. Actually, the time of the abandonment of all of the main centers does not fall between these two dates. Some were deserted prior to the beginning of the great drought and a few continued to be occupied after the dry period had begun.

One of the most interesting theories yet advanced is based on the suggestion that a really severe drought was not necessary to upset the economy of the Pueblo farmers.[10][39] Some dry farming was practiced and there was some ditch irrigation, but the greatest dependence seems to have been on flood-water farming in valley bottoms. This is a system whereby water is simply diverted and distributed through the fields when floods come down the valley. During periods when rainfall is deficient, although not sufficiently so to warrant the use of the term drought, steep channels, known as arroyos, are cut into flood plains; the water-table is lowered, and flood-water fields become useless. Not only may the fields themselves be dissected by the arroyo cutting, but water can no longer be diverted for flood irrigation. If, as seems probable, the great drought was only the climax of a period of increasing dryness when much farmland was lost through arroyo-cutting, it is not hard to understand why the Pueblo farmers might move on to more favored localities.

Another theory advanced to explain the departure of the ancient agriculturists, and one which has enthusiastic supporters, is that they were driven from their homes by fierce nomadic tribes who were attracted by the wealth of food stored in their granaries.[73] Much of this thinking is based on what we know of nomadic raids in general, and the records of the terrible Navajo and Apache depredations from the middle of the seventeenth century until their comparatively recent subjugation by the United States Army. For years it has been the practice simply to accept the belief that fierce warlike tribes had preyed on the peaceful Pueblos for centuries. More recently, however, some searching questions have been asked, and this theory is under close scrutiny.[80]

It is granted that the type of construction employed in the Great-Pueblo era indicates some need for defense, but it does not show against whom the defense was needed. Assuming that there were nomadic tribesmen, ready and anxious to carry away the patiently accumulated wealth of the Pueblos, we must ask ourselves what advantage they would have had over their victims which would have enabled them to carry out their depredations. If the nomads had been mounted, as they were in later times, they would have had the advantages of speed and mobility which are essential for surprise attacks—the only type which would be of much avail against a heavily fortified structure. Only much later, however, were horses introduced into the Southwest; and at this time the attackers would have had to travel on foot.

Greater numbers, or superior organization, might have given them an advantage, but we can hardly believe that the nomads were as numerous or had as good an organization as that of the people of the Pueblos. The region in which they presumably lived would certainly not support a large population, and particularly one with an essentially parasitic economy which did not produce. With such an economy, people cannot live too close together without exhausting the available resources, and a thinly spread population is unlikely to be highly organized.

Great physical superiority may be another factor in the winning of battles between people who have not yet become so civilized as to have machines which will enable one individual to kill thousands of his fellow men. Any physical superiority, however, would seem to rest with the sedentary people who had an assured food supply. Moreover, their life was still sufficiently rugged so that there can hardly be any question of their having been greatly weakened by soft living.

Doubtless, there were sporadic raids by nomads, and these may have had a cumulative effect in upsetting Pueblo economy. The role played by periods of arroyo-cutting and by droughts can certainly not be overlooked. These may well have done more than reduce the food supply. When food is scarce, raids are more likely to occur, and it is entirely probable that the relationship between various groups deteriorated as prosperity decreased. Toward the end of Great-Pueblo times we find increasing signs of warfare in the form of burned buildings and unburied bodies, many of which show evidence of violence. The latter are of the characteristic Pueblo type, however, and would seem to indicate warfare between people of the same blood.

The most logical theory seems to be that many factors contributed to the great change which occurred in the Anasazi province. Doubtless, climatic conditions were the great underlying cause, but there may

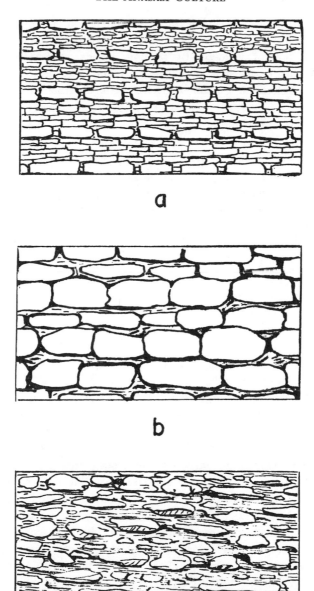

Fig. 28—Types of Great-Pueblo masonry. a. Chaco,
b. Mesa Verde, c. Kayenta.

have been others. We cannot afford to confine our attention entirely
to material causes, but must take into consideration even the possibility that fears, engendered by religious beliefs, may have played a
part. All this, however, is largely in the realm of conjecture, for, with
no written records, there can be no first hand information.

Whatever the causes, the end of the Great-Pueblo period was
marked by a redistribution of population and a general trend toward
concentration in places where conditions were most favorable. While
the chief movement was from the north, there was also some with-
drawing from the south. By the beginning of the following period,
which is sometimes known as the *Regressive-Pueblo* phase, much territory throughout the Plateau area was deserted. Main population centers
were confined to the central area of the Plateau. This includes the Little
Colorado drainage, particularly the section in the vicinity of the
Hopi mesas and the Zuñi region, and the Rio Grande drainage.

Although there were certain traits which characterized the culture
as a whole during the Great-Pueblo period, there was a somewhat
different development in each of the three main culture centers which
flourished at this time. In each of these there was an intense local
specialization in architecture and in pottery making.

The latter, in fact, became so highly specialized that products of
the various areas may be identified no matter where they may be
found. No two pieces of pottery of each kind will be exactly alike,
but they all conform to a common ideal. It must be stressed that,
by *culture center*, we do not mean an entirely restricted area, but
rather a nuclear section in which specialization was most intense and
from which influence spread, often over a large area.

The oldest settlement, and one which continued to be a cultural
leader with far-reaching influences for centuries, lies in the Chaco
Canyon of New Mexico.[61] [73] [95] The Chaco River is a tributary of the
San Juan which flows through northwestern New Mexico. Within the
canyon are found twelve large ruins, which include some of the most
spectacular of the ancient buildings erected in North America, and
innumerable smaller ruins. The twelve great communal buildings were
more or less rectangular, oval, or D-shaped structures, with up to four
stories on three sides, and a single-storied row of rooms which bowed
out to the southeast. Within the walls was a great open court or plaza
which contained numerous kivas. Other kivas were incorporated within
the building mass. It is interesting to note that the traditional underground character of the ceremonial chamber was preserved through

Fig. 29—Pueblo Bonito, Chaco Canyon National Monument, New Mexico. (Courtesy National Park Service.)

filling in the space between the circular walls of the kiva and the straight walls of the other rooms.

One of the largest and most famous Chacoan structures is called Pueblo Bonito.[71] It was a town, consisting of a single building, which covered over three acres of ground and contained at least eight hundred rooms. It has been estimated that it could have sheltered 1200 inhabitants, and it was the largest "apartment house" in the world until a larger one was erected in New York in 1882. Building had begun at Pueblo Bonito as early as 919 A.D., but it did not reach its final form until 1067 A.D. or later. It is believed that the more definitely planned settlement may have been the work of new and more progressive people who moved into the area.

Pueblo Bonito, as it stands today after archaeologists have cleared away the dust of centuries and exposed it to view, is truly a remarkable structure. Even in ruins, it is not too difficult to picture it as it must have been during those long ago times when it was one of the great cultural centers of the Southwest. On three sides of the center court was the main building, terraced back from a one-story level in front to four stories in the rear. With each succeeding row of rooms the height was increased by one story. Extending from the ends and enclosing the side to the south was a one-story row of rooms. Outside of this single tier was the rubbish heap around which retaining walls were built. The center court contained numerous kivas, and others were incorporated in the building mass.

In addition to the regular kivas, whose diameter rarely exceeded twenty-five feet, there have also been found in Chaco Canyon, Aztec, and other sites with Chacoan architecture, big circular structures with diameters of from forty to sixty feet ringed by a concentric row of small rooms. These are known as *Great Kivas*. They are thought to have been religious edifices which served an entire community, while the smaller kivas probably belonged to various clans or societies. Great Kivas, though in a simpler form, were apparently present as far back as Modified-Basketmaker times when most rites were performed in dwellings, but a larger place was needed for ceremonies in which the people of a whole community or district participated.

Architecture in general reached its highest development in Chaco Canyon, and there was real beauty as well as solidity of construction. The walls were massive, although there was a decrease in thickness with succeeding stories, as the weight resting upon them was reduced. The most distinctive type of masonry consisted of a center portion of stone and adobe or rubble, faced on two sides by a veneer of horizontally laid thin, tabular stones. These are so perfectly fitted together that a knife blade can scarcely be inserted between them. Sometimes this particular type of stone was not available and it was necessary to use more massively bedded stones which had to be dressed to the proper shape, but the masonry was uniformly good. Great beams, stripped of bark and beautifully dressed, were placed across the chambers. Small poles, which were finished with equal care, were placed at right angles to the main beams and so spaced as to form patterns. Over these lay carefully fashioned mats of peeled willow, followed by a cedar splint layer. A thick coat of earth overlay the entire mass, forming a floor for the room above as well as a roof for the one below.

The use of big logs, which do not bear the scars indicative of transportation over a long distance, and the common use of willow, which must have been abundant, suggest conditions different from those of today. It is not known with certainty whether there has been a real climatic change. Many believe that, when hoofed animals were introduced by the white man, the grass cover was destroyed, and that this led to the cutting of arroyos which carried off flood waters and lowered the underground seepage and as a result the land became progressively drier, but others believe that there were earlier periods of arroyo-cutting.

Although severe erosion did not occur until a later time, it was a process with which the ancient inhabitants of Pueblo Bonito were familiar. Overlooking the Pueblo was a tremendous rock with an estimated weight of 30,000 tons, detached from the cliff and seeming so precariously balanced as to threaten the building. At the foot of the rock the prehistoric inhabitants erected a brace of wood and stone masonry. At first glance it seems a rather pathetic effort, but actually it may not show any ignorance on the part of the ancient Bonitians, but rather a familiarity with certain engineering principles which suggested that protecting the base of the rock would curtail erosion and help to prevent the threatened disaster. The fears of the prehistoric inhabitants were never realized in their time, for it was not until January 22, 1941, that the threatening rock finally fell. It damaged one hundred feet of the back wall of the pueblo and twenty-one adjacent rooms.

Rooms in Chaco-Canyon structures were relatively large and high ceilinged, with plastered walls. The inner rooms, which lacked light and air, were used for storage. Household activities were not confined to the rooms, for the roofs of the lower tiers provided additional living space, and much work, such as the preparing of food, the making of pottery, and the flaking of arrowheads, probably took place in the open. Fire places are rare in the rooms, and it seems likely that much of the cooking was done outside—in the courts and on the roofs. At first there were doorways and high windows in the outer wall, but these were later blocked off with masonry. The single gateway in the front of the pueblo was first greatly narrowed and then entirely closed, so that the great house could be entered only by means of a ladder which,

Fig. 30—Chaco black-on-white pottery of the Great-Pueblo period. (Courtesy The American Museum of Natural History; Taylor Museum photograph.)

if necessary, could be withdrawn. This is some of the best evidence of the fear of attack which must have existed.

In its own way, pottery reached as high a point of development as did architecture. The main wares were black-on-white and corrugated. The former was thin and hard, usually a good white, but sometimes a light gray. Designs were, for the most part, hatchured patterns with the thin filling lines surrounded by heavier boundary lines. Band decorations were widely used. Bowls, pitchers, and ladles were the most usual shapes, but cylindrical vases and effigy pots with human figures were not unknown. The cooking ware was corrugated and usually consisted of large jars with wide mouths. This pottery was very well made, with attractive patterns produced by making sharp, clear-cut, indentations in the corrugations. Some red pottery has also been found.

Neither the architecture nor the pottery which we refer to as being of the Chaco-Canyon type was limited to the narrow confines of the canyon itself. They are also represented in such places as the great ruin at Aztec, New Mexico,[94] and at various other sites in the San Juan area. In some cases, particularly in northeastern Arizona, architecture was Chacoan in character, but pottery was not.

At Chaco Canyon, and in other Great-Pueblo centers, various minor arts also flourished. Feather cloth continued to be made, and still provided robes and blankets for the living and wrappings for the dead. Flocks of domesticated turkeys were kept to provide feathers, and parrots and other brilliantly colored birds were brought from the south. Cotton fabrics were steadily increasing in importance. Some large blankets were woven which must have required the use of an upright loom. Colored yarns were used, and there was some painting of finished fabrics. Variations in weaving also provided decoration. There is no evidence that the people wore any tailored garments, but the remains of a poncho with a slit for the head has been found. There were also some garments of dressed buckskin, in addition to those of feather and cotton cloth.

Some sandals with notched toes were woven of fine cord, but this art had degenerated and decoration was less elaborate, both as regards colored and raised patterns. Most sandals were of plaited yucca leaves, and many had square toes. Twined-weaving does not seem to have survived. Coiled baskets were still produced, but they were not plentiful. They were of a finer weave than those of the preceding periods but had fewer colored designs. Yucca ring baskets were extremely common. These were made by fastening the outer edges of a bowl-shaped mat, made of twilled yucca leaves, over a wooden ring. Twilled mats of rushes or reeds, were made in quantity and were widely used as floor and roof coverings. Tubular pipes were made of both clay and stone. These are rarely found whole, and it is thought they may have been intentionally broken—possibly to avoid profanation after use in sacred rites.

It was in the field of ornaments that the minor arts of the Chaco people reached their highest development. Olivella-shell beads were still widely used, and there were also stone beads and stone and shell pendants carved into the form of birds and animals; but it was turquoise which provided the material for the finest ornaments. Some beautiful mosaics were made of turquoise, and it was also used in the making of beads. One incomparable necklace found at Pueblo Bonito contained twenty-five hundred beads and four pendants of magnificent sky blue stones.[71] All were shaped and polished with a skill that would do credit to a modern jeweller with all his highly specialized tools. An unbelievable amount of work must have gone into the production of such an ornament when only stone tools were available. Unfortunately we do not have many such specimens—due to the mystery which surrounds the final disposition of the remains of the ancient inhabitants of Pueblo Bonito.

Although burials are commonly found in the refuse heaps associated with the small dwellings of Chaco Canyon, the majority of the dead of the great communal houses have never been found. Occasional burials have been found but not enough to account for even five per cent of the deaths which must have occurred during the period of occupation. Many of the graves which have been found in abandoned rooms had already been looted by pre-archaeological grave robbers. The few undisturbed interments which have been discovered suggest that grave offerings were extremely rich, and, with such an incentive, archaeologists have searched far and wide for the ancient cemeteries, but, as yet, without success. There is no indication that cremation was practiced, so there is still hope that some day we may find the spot where the ancient people laid the dead to rest, and so learn more of their arts and crafts.

Some idea of the remarkable finds which may yet be made may be gained from a burial found in Ridge Ruin, a Great-Pueblo site about twenty miles east of Flagstaff, Arizona.[88] Here was found the body of a man interred with over six hundred articles, many of which show the most remarkable workmanship. They included pottery, beautiful baskets, fine turquoise mosaics, stone and shell ornaments, and hundreds of finely flaked arrowheads. This was of course an unusual burial, and many of the offerings were ceremonial objects such as would be placed in a grave only under extraordinary circumstances, but it gives some idea of the wealth of material which may yet be found and which will contribute to our knowledge of the ancient Pueblo culture.

The great dwellings of Chaco Canyon apparently were abandoned in the twelfth century, and there is no doubt a fascinating story connected with the abandonment of these huge buildings which were erected with so much labor and finished with such care. It is a story which we do not yet fully understand, and, to a great extent, we can only guess at the causes which underlay the migration. It was probably the first phase of the general movement which eventually involved the entire population of the northern part of the Southwest, but it is even more difficult to account for than some of the later migrations, for there were no particularly severe droughts at this time. There were some dry years, however, which may have led to disastrous arroyo-cutting.

Some of the most famous of all buildings of this period are those of Mesa Verde, [73] [95] whose location in high cliffs has led to the use of the name "Cliff Dwellers" for the people who lived here from the middle of the eleventh century until the latter part of the thirteenth. Mesa Verde is a large plateau in the drainage of the Mancos River in southwestern Colorado. Here in great, high caves, protected by massive sandstone overhangs, but open to the sun, were built huge houses which were really cities. These pueblos were in many essentials like those of Chaco Canyon and other open sites, but they seem to have grown by accretion rather than according to a fixed plan, and the shape of the structures was largely determined by that of the caves which sheltered them.

There are certain unmistakable differences between the architecture and pottery of Chaco Canyon and of Mesa Verde. As in the case of the Chaco culture, Mesa Verde traits were not confined to the type locality, but had a far-reaching influence. Numerous ruins with the same basic characteristics, but not necessarily in caves, are found along the Mancos River and for some distance to the east and to the west. After the abandonment of the Mesa Verde proper, the influence became quite important in the south.

At Mesa Verde walls were thinner than in the Chacoan houses. This can probably be traced to the material used, as well as to the fact that the cave ceilings somewhat limited the height of the buildings, and with the reduced strain, thick walls were not needed. Flat tabular stones were not available, and walls were constructed of massive stone which was shaped into large, loaflike, blocks by pecking. Walls were of solid rock with no center fill of rubble or earth, and little mortar was used.

Of the many ruins in Mesa Verde National Park the most famous, and also the largest, is Cliff Palace.[125] With its many rooms and great stone towers it does give the impression of a palace, but this is of course a misnomer. Far from being the palace of a ruler, it was the home of

Fig. 31—Cliff Palace, Mesa Verde National Park, Colorado.

hundreds of farmers and their families. Cliff Palace is a terraced building reaching to four stories in height in some places and containing over two hundred rooms and twenty-three kivas. The rooms were small, often irregularly shaped, and had low ceilings. Not all of them were used as living quarters. Some were used for storage. Storage must have been of great importance, since grain designed for winter food, as well as seed corn, had to be preserved. Also, it is probable that these ancient farmers accumulated large reserves to tide them over years when the crops failed, as do their present-day descendants. Other rooms contained boxlike structures of stone slabs which held metates, and these are thought to have been milling rooms in which the corn was ground. The living rooms, each one occupied by one family, were small and probably none too comfortable.

Some rooms were entered through the roofs but others had doors and windows. Even when doors were present, they were small and high above the floor and were probably reached by ladders. Few of the rooms contained fireplaces. The smoke from a fire in a small room with inadequate ventilation would present a definite problem, but life in the winter in an unheated room in a high canyon would not seem particularly appealing to present-day Americans. The walls of the houses were neatly plastered, sometimes colored and sometimes embellished by well painted designs.

The small size of the rooms has often given rise to a belief that the inhabitants were abnormally small. Actually the people were of normal size, but they probably did not spend much time in the rooms. Much of the life of the great house must have centered about the open courts and terraced roofs. When the men were not working in the fields or hunting on the mesa tops, they must have spent much time in their kivas, which may have served as habitations for the unmarried men and general meeting places, as well as providing a setting for the religious rites. While we cannot be sure what these ceremonies were, it seems certain that they were concerned with the well-being of the crops, which must be the first concern of all farmers, and that their form and content must have been greatly influenced by the ever present need of water which has always dominated life in the Southwest.

Most of the kivas were small circular structures, about thirteen feet in diameter, with the wall set back a foot or more, some three feet above the floor, to form an encircling bench. On this bench were six masonry pilasters which helped to support a cribbed roof. The spaces between pilasters formed recesses. The one to the south was the deepest and contained the ventilator flue. The deflector, which stood between it and the center fire pit, was usually of masonry, but sometimes of wattle work. In addition to these circular kivas, which were the normal type, there were also circular or rectangular rooms with rounded corners which seem to have had a ceremonial nature, although they lacked the usual kiva features and were not subterranean, though surrounded by high walls. For the most part kivas lay in the front of the cave, but there were also some in the rear.

In addition to the various rooms and kivas there were also towers, sometimes incorporated in the building-mass of the great house, and sometimes built separately. They had various shapes, including round, oval, D-shaped, and rectangular. Some were two stories high. There were doorways in the side, but no windows. There are many theories as to the use of these towers, but there are some objections to all of them. One is, that they were designed as observation posts to watch for enemies, or as fortresses. They are usually loop-holed and, when found at a distance from the dwelling, are often on easily defended points which command a good view of the adjoining terrain. This, however, is not invariably the case, for some of the isolated towers are so placed that there would be little visibility, and defense would be extremely difficult. Many are far too small to have served as fortresses. Another theory is that they may have had some ceremonial use, and may have served as solar observatories to obtain calendrical data essential in the planting and harvesting of crops and fixing of dates for religious rites connected with these activities. Some, however, are located in spots not suitable for making such observations.

Across the canyon from Cliff Palace is a remarkable surface-structure known as "Sun Temple", which some archaeologists consider an elaborate form of tower. This is an unroofed D-shaped building with double walls over twelve feet high. The space between the walls is divided into small rooms, and there are ten other rooms at the west end of the building. There is one kiva in this western section and two others in the big center court enclosed by the walls.

Life in Mesa Verde, as in all the Pueblo area, depended on agriculture. There was dry farming on the mesa tops, but irrigation was particularly well developed here.[7] A broad, shallow ditch, some four miles long, and with a very regular gradient has been found on the Mesa Verde. Apparently water was turned out on the cornfields from this ditch. There were also check dams which caught the run-off of heavy summer rains and made it available for the crops. They served a further purpose in conserving soil which might otherwise have been washed away. Reservoirs were present and must have also provided water for the fields, but they have not yet been studied sufficiently for us to have much information as to their construction or use.

Mesa Verde pottery is as distinctive as its architecture. Fine corrugated vessels were made, and a small percentage of imported red pottery was present, but the outstanding ware was black-on-white. This pottery has certain distinctive features which make it easy to recognize. The walls are fairly thick, and rims tend to be square and flat. The background is a pearly white with grayish undertones. Most vessels have been so carefully polished that they have a glossy surface which sometimes almost gives an impression of translucence. The decoration, applied with black paint, is usually in the form of geometric patterns, although a few bowls show life-forms in their designs. Band patterns were extremely common, and many large solid elements as well as hatchured patterns were used. The latter tend to be much coarser than those on Chaco pottery. The most distinctive forms were flat-bottomed mugs, which resemble beer steins, and "kiva jars." The latter are vessels in the form of a somewhat flattened sphere, with fitted covers resting on an inner rim, as do those of modern sugar bowls. There were also many bowls, ollas (water jars), ladles, canteens, and seed jars.

Fig. 32—Mesa Verde black-on-white pottery of the Great-Pueblo period.
(Courtesy Mesa Verde National Park.)

The minor arts of Mesa Verde seem to have been much like those of Chaco Canyon, but neither material nor craftsmanship appears to have been as good. Again, the scarcity of burials has reduced the chances of obtaining much valuable information. In open sites they have been found occasionally in refuse heaps, but more often they occur in pits under floors of houses which continued to be occupied, or in abandoned rooms. At Mesa Verde a few burials have been found in refuse heaps behind the houses, a few under the floors of abandoned rooms, and others in the cracks and crevices of the talus slope in front of the caves. There is also some evidence of occasional cremations.[24] On mesa tops, have been found a few stone rings overlying calcined human bones, and one room in Cliff Palace was found to contain ashes and human bones. There is no evidence, however, that cremation was widely practiced, and the few graves which have been found would account for only a small fraction of the deaths which must have occurred during the period of occupancy. It is believed probable that most burials may have been in the refuse heaps in front of the caves and that they have weathered away.

The last building date we have for Mesa Verde is 1273, but it is possible that the great houses may have been occupied for some time after this. The final date of departure probably falls within the period of the disastrous drought of 1276 to 1299, when the farmers of Mesa Verde must have been fighting a losing battle against overwhelming odds. The departure seems to have been an orderly one, for the people took most of their possessions with them. There does not seem to have been any one, great migration. Rather it appears that first one section, and then another, was abandoned as one or more small groups moved on. The abandonment of the cliff houses has given rise to many fantastic stories, and there has grown up a certain belief that the "Cliff Dwellers" more or less disappeared into thin air. Certainly there is enough mystery connected with this strange departure, but great numbers of people do not simply vanish. Actually, they moved farther and farther south, and perhaps to the southeast and southwest, looking for more favorable locations. As they mingled with other groups they lost their identity, but doubtless there is still a strain of Mesa Verde blood in the present Pueblo Indian population. Perhaps the Indian, whom we see selling jewelry in the lobby of some modern Southwestern hotel, had ancestors who helped build the ancient city which we know as Cliff Palace.

In addition to sites which were occupied by people with a Chacoan culture and those inhabited by people with Mesa Verde affiliations, there are others which show both influences at different periods. Lowry Ruin,[81] not far from Mesa Verde in southwestern Colorado, contains a Pueblo and a Great Kiva with Chacoan Masonry. The early pottery was not entirely like that found in sites in the Chaco Canyon itself, but closely resembled it. It must be emphasized that *Chacoan* is simply a term which refers to a generalized culture, and not just to the sites of the type locality. In the top portion of the fill of some rooms at Lowry Ruin is found Mesa Verde black-on-white pottery. It is not known whether this indicates the presence of Mesa Verde people, or if only the pottery, or perhaps even the technique, was introduced. We do know, however, that Lowry Pueblo was occupied, abandoned, and then reoccupied a number of times from the time when it was first built, late in the eleventh century, until it was finally deserted, about the middle of the twelfth century. This is one of the sites which does much to upset certain theories as to the causes of the abandonment of the northern frontier. It was not prepared for defense, and had entrances on the ground level, and there is no indication of any violence. Final abandonment came long before the great drought of 1276 to 1299.

An even more famous site is that of Aztec,[94] now a National Monument, which lies one mile north of the town of Aztec, New Mexico. Here were built a big communal house and Great Kiva with Chacoan masonry. The ground plans were almost identical with those of Chettro Kettle, one of the important structures of Chaco Canyon. The main building was in the shape of a square "U", with an arc-shaped row of rooms in front. More famous than the Pueblo itself is the "House of the Great Kiva." This remarkable structure was essentially circular, and consisted of a large kiva surrounded by a concentric ring of arc-shaped surface-rooms. The kiva, which was encircled by two benches or shelves, was forty-one feet across at floor level and forty-eight feet in diameter at the level of the second bench. In the floor were two large, masonry-lined, sub-floor vaults and a masonry box, midway between the south ends of the vaults, which is believed to have been a fire altar. The twelve rooms surrounding the kiva are not stained and littered, as are the usual living quarters, so it seems certain that they were strictly ceremonial chambers. On the south side is an alcove, opening directly into the kiva, which is thought to have been a shrine room. A rectangle of masonry in the center of the alcove was presumably a permanent altar.

Some of the living rooms in the pueblo bear evidence of Mesa Verde workmanship, and almost 95% of the pottery is of the Mesa Verde type. This gave rise to the belief that Aztec was a hybrid settlement of people of both cultures. Excavation proved that the explanation was not quite so simple. The original builders of the Pueblo and Great Kiva had Chacoan connections. They occupied the Pueblo for many years, then, taking their possessions with them, they moved away. Why they left, or where they went, we do not know. For a long time

Fig. 33—Betatakin, Navajo National Monument, Arizona. (Courtesy National Park Service.)

the Pueblo was abandoned, then a group of Mesa Verde people arrived and moved in. They changed and modified many of the rooms
in accordance with their own customs. The rooms which they built
were smaller and the masonry was of the typical Mesa Verde type,
as was the pottery. After this immigration the great house was occupied for a long time. At first the people were quite prosperous, but
eventually there came a period of depression and disintegration. Building techniques became progressively worse, and there was an equal
deterioration in pottery making. Living quarters were no longer
cleaned. Many women and children died, and, when they were buried
few, if any, mortuary offerings were placed with them. The end came
when the pueblo was intentionally fired and destroyed. Whether this
was done by the people themselves, or by enemies who attacked them
when they were no longer able to defend themselves, we do not know.

In the vicinity of Kayenta, Arizona, which lies to the south of the
San Juan and west of both Mesa Verde and Chaco Canyon, was a third
cultural center with far-reaching influences.[3][73] Here are found both
cliff houses and pueblos in the open. Two of the largest and most
famous cliff dwellings are Keet Seel and Betatakin. These were among
the last of the great houses of the San Juan area to be occupied. Tree-
ring dates for Betatakin range between 1260 and 1277, and those for
Keet Seel between 1274 and 1284. By the latter date the remainder of
the northern frontier had been almost entirely deserted.

The masonry throughout was quite inferior. It was somewhat
better in the open sites, which were characterized by loose aggregations
of houses, than in the cliff houses. On the whole, masonry was marked
by the use of irregularly shaped stones, inaccurate coursing, and the
use of great quantities of adobe mortar. Also, wattlework walls, that is,
walls formed of upright poles through which were interwoven smaller
sticks, were quite common. One of the chief differences between the
Kayenta area and other cultural centers lies in the kivas. In open
sites and in some cliff houses, of which Bat Woman House is a good
example, only circular kivas are found, but they lack the pilasters
characteristic of such structures in other sections. At Keet Seel there
are some kivas, but many of the ceremonial structures are of another
type, sometimes called *kihus*. These are square above-ground chambers
which contain the characteristic fire pits and deflectors of kivas, but
have a door instead of an air shaft. At Betatakin this is the only type
of ceremonial room.

Pottery from this area differs in many respects from that of the eastern sites. Corrugated pottery was made, but it displays poorer workmanship and less graceful shapes than examples from Chaco and Mesa Verde. Black-on-white ware was excellent, with a good paste and a clear slip. The decoration is fine and quite distinctive. Elaborate patterns, primarily interlocking keys, frets, and spirals, were used. The elements, painted in black, are so close together and so heavy that little of the white background shows and a negative design results, giving

Fig. 34—Black-on-white pottery from the Kayenta area. Great-Pueblo period. (Courtesy Museum of Northern Arizona.)

the impression of a white design on a black background. What little of the white background does appear is often hatched or cross-hatched, giving what has been described as a "mosquito bar" effect. The principal forms were ollas, bowls, and ladles. Seed jars and small handled jugs were also made, but they were not as common. An important form was the colander, a type of utensil which was confined to this culture.

The most distinctive Kayenta pottery was a polychrome ware on which, as the name implies, multiple colors were used. The base color was orange or yellow, and designs were applied in black, red, and white paint. There was a wide use of broad, red bands outlined in black or in black and white. Coarse hatchures divided into groups, with other design elements between the groups, were quite common. There was an abundance of this ware, although bowls and small handled jugs were the only forms represented.

Very few burials have been found in the cliff houses. A small number have been uncovered in unoccupied sections of the caves, in the talus slope in front, and in small shelters nearby. In open sites closely flexed bodies accompanied by mortuary pottery have been found in oval pits dug in the rubbish heaps.

Although attention is naturally centered on the San Juan region, where the Great Pueblo culture had its most spectacular development and where the most extensive excavations have been carried on, the remainder of the Plateau Province cannot be overlooked.

Sixteen miles from Zuñi, in the Little Colorado drainage, is a famous site, known as the "Village of the Great Kivas."[108] Here were found three communal dwellings and two Great Kivas. Of the latter, only one has been excavated. It was bordered with rooms but had no true peripheral chambers. Both are larger than the Great Kiva at Aztec. The one which has been excavated is fifty-one feet in diameter, and the unexcavated one is seventy-five feet across. In addition to these structures and some small kivas associated with the largest building, there were two rectangular rooms with kiva features. These are similar to the fraternity chambers used in Zuñi at the present time. The construction of the village was begun in the eleventh century by people with a Chacoan culture. After a time, due to the arrival of new people, the community increased in size. It is thought that these people came from the south, possibly from the Upper Gila region.

To the west, in what we now know as the Hopi country, good-sized Pueblos were being constructed. There was much black-on-white and gray corrugated pottery and, in the latter part of the period, fine pottery with black designs on an orange background was made. Kivas were rectangular or D-shaped. To the south and east of this region a particularly fine polychrome ware was being made. Black and white designs were applied on an orange-red background.

Still farther south, in the vicinity of Fort Apache, Arizona, is Kinishba, a Great-Pueblo site occupied between 1050 and 1350 A. D. It combined three pueblos, of which two have been excavated. The main building is an irregularly rectangular structure, built around a big central court, which seems to have grown by accretion rather than according to fixed plan. The masonry was not particularly good. The stones were not carefully shaped, and there was an extensive use of mortar. Many fine ornaments were made. Kinishba appears to have been something of a trade center, and pottery characteristic of many different areas is found here. One distinctive type of pottery which was made locally was a polychrome ware with red and black designs on a buff background.

The Rio Grande drainage, to the east, did not become a very important province until the following period, but there is evidence of the presence of a scattered population as far back as Developmental-Pueblo times. Eventually, migrations from the north brought in many new people. Prior to that time architecture was not highly developed. There was little coursed masonry, but extensive use of adobe. Some rather inferior black on white pottery of a generalized type and a poor corrugated ware were manufactured, and a little black-on-red pottery was imported.

In the Mimbres drainage of southwestern New Mexico, lived a group of people who, during the Great-Pueblo Period, made some of the most remarkable pottery that has ever been produced. Although they are often considered as part of the Anasazi, much of their development was due to two other cultures as well. Because of this, discussion of the Mimbres people and their achievements will be postponed until the other cultures have been considered.

The Largo-Gallina Phase

In the Largo drainage of north-central New Mexico some extremely interesting remains of a Pueblolike people have been found.[91] Chronologically they fit into Great-Pueblo times, but they are not entirely Anasazi in culture. The name *Largo* has been given to this cultural phase. Tree-ring dates have been obtained in Largo sites, and it is possible to place the period of occupation as extending from the beginning of the twelfth to the middle of the thirteenth century.

The inhabitants of these sites lived in both pit and surface houses. These structures are relatively large. The latter have massive walls of uncoursed masonry up to four feet thick. All dwellings contained low-walled storage bins. Although more evidence will be needed before definite conclusions may be reached, it seems possible to show a definite architectural development from pit houses to the thick walled surface houses of uncoursed masonry which were followed by others with coursed masonry walls. Other, presumably later, structures may be described as small pueblos, but these have not yet been thoroughly investigated.

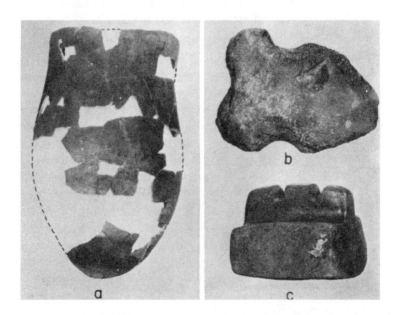

Fig. 35—Above, Largo surface house. Below, Largo artifacts,
a. pointed-bottomed pot, b. axe, c. arrow-shaft smoother.
(Courtesy Laboratory of Anthropology.)

Black-on-white pottery, which was Puebloan in character, was made, but most of the utility ware was unlike anything made elsewhere by the Anasazi. These vessels had pointed bottoms and were decorated with fillets at the rim or just below. They were not scraped, but were smoothed by holding a mushroom-shaped object inside the vessel, while it was still plastic, and striking the exterior with a wooden paddle. This is known as the *paddle-and-anvil* technique. These vessels resemble Woodland pottery from the eastern United States and Navajo cooking pots.

Other distinctive artifacts included axes of a triple-notched type which required a T-shaped hafting, arrow-shaft smoothers, and elbow-shaped pipes. The smoothers are large pieces of fine grained rock with deep grooves in which arrow shafts were rubbed in the process of shaping them. On the bowls of the pipes were two little leglike projections which served to provide a base when they were not in use. There was an extensive use of antler.

To the east of the Largo country and on the other side of the continental divide are found similar sites which represent the same culture. This phase has been called the *Gallina*.[63] Both phases are often considered together and referred to as the *Largo-Gallina*.

In the Gallina country there is the same combination of pit houses and surface structures as in the Largo sites. Most sites are in good defensive positions, but this is not true of all of them. Sites usually consist of three or four house units grouped together, although single houses also have been found. Most of these dwellings are towerlike structures, square in outline but with rounded corners. They range from eighteen to twenty feet in diameter and have walls still standing to a height of from twelve to seventeen feet. These walls were extraordinarily massive, being in some cases as much as six feet thick. House interiors were characterized by flagstone floors and the wide use of storage bins with sandstone covers. The bins were usually on the south side. In most houses, there was an adobe bench encircling the northern part of the room. Fine murals had been painted above the bench in one house. On the whole, these structures resemble square kivas to which bins have been added, although they were used as homes and not as ceremonial chambers. Roofs consisted of a pole and adobe foundation with flagstones providing a shingled effect. Entrance appears to have been through the roof which, due to the great height of the buildings, must have been reached by ladders or platforms. In addition to the towerlike buildings there are also pit houses which are found in conjunction with them.

Anasazi traits include twilled yucca sandals, coiled basketry, feather-cloth, twined-bags, and black-on-white pottery. Axes, shaft-smoothers, and pipes, resemble those found in Largo sites and the cooking pots with the pointed bottoms are the same. Chisel-like objects made of deer and elk antler and unusual stone knives were also found. The latter were leaf-shaped blades with notches in the sides close to the center. One end was pointed and the other somewhat blunted. It is the latter end which seems to have been used while the pointed end was hafted.

In general, the Largo-Gallina seems to be a Pueblo phase, probably derived from the Rosa phase [41] of the Governador area, which was subjected to foreign influences, probably from the north. Similarities between Largo-Gallina and Navajo utility vessels may indicate some relationship.

Athapaskan People

We may next consider the problem of the Navajos and Apaches who figured so prominently in Southwestern history. They are relative newcomers in the area and it is only within recent years that they have stirred the interest of many archaeologists, although the Navajos have been literally haunted by ethnologists for a long time.

Both Navajos and Apaches speak dialects of the Athapaskan language which is spoken by many groups in northwestern Canada. At some time in the relatively recent past, groups of Athapaskan-speaking people left their northern homeland and drifted southward, some going along the coast and others wandering farther east. Some reached the Southwest and the descendants of these migrants are the Indians whom we know as Navajos and Apaches.

There are many theories as to the route which they followed. Recent finds, in the Colorado Rockies, of circular structures of dry-laid masonry which are non-Pueblo in character and which resemble certain Navajo houses or hogans, suggest that at least some of the migrants may have followed the main mountain ranges.[68] It is also possible that they may have moved south through the Great Basin west of the Rocky Mountains, or along the High Plains east of the mountains. Pottery finds give 1100 A. D. as the earliest date for the hoganlike structures in the Colorado mountains. It is not certain that these houses were built by Athapaskan people, however, and there is no definite knowledge as to just when the Athapaskans reached the Southwest and first came into contact with the Pueblo Indians. The earliest tree-ring date yet obtained in the Pueblo area from any site which we may be sure is Navajo is from the Governador area and falls in the middle of the sixteenth century.[40] If the Navajos arrived as early as 1200 A.D. they may have influenced the Largo-Gallina people and have been influenced by them, but this is still a moot question. A relatively early arrival might also aid in explaining the withdrawal of the Pueblos from the northern area.

SUMMARY

We may summarize the Great-Pueblo period as follows. It was the period in which the Anasazi culture attained its highest development, and it was marked by intense local specialization. Most of the basic aspects of the culture had already been well established, but there was tremendous improvement and amplification. Unit houses continued to be occupied throughout the period but there was a general coalescence of the population. The trend was toward concentration in great, terraced communal houses, up to five stories in height, and large enough to shelter hundreds of people. Some were built in the open and others in large natural caverns in cliffs. Small kivas, presumably used by small groups such as clans, were incorporated in the houses or placed in the central court. There were also Great Kivas, larger and more elaborate structures, believed to have served an entire community. There was local variation in architectural details, both as regards masonry types and house structures.

Pottery was remarkably fine and designs were often quite elaborate. There was such specialization that the products of various centers are readily distinguished. Culinary ware was corrugated. Among the decorated types, black-on-white predominated but there was some black-on-red ware and some black bowls with red interiors, and in the Kayenta district and farther south polychrome pottery was widely made. Late in the period black-on-orange wares became important in the Little Colorado drainage.

Much progress was made in the weaving of cotton cloth. Ornaments were highly developed and turquoise was widely used. Remarkable mosaics as well as beads and pendants were manufactured. Some coiled baskets were still made but yucca ring baskets were the leading type.

Although it is only in the realm of material culture that we have concrete evidence, there can be little doubt that the heights reached in the production of material things must have been reflected in the whole life of the people. There is every reason to believe that an essentially democratic form of government prevailed, but communal living must have required a high degree of organization. Doubtless religion played a great part in the life of the community and had far-reaching influences.

In the latter part of the thirteenth century, the Southwest seems to have had a dry period, marked by arroyo cutting that destroyed farmland, which was followed by a disastrous drought. These factors, with possible raids by nomadic warriors, internal discord, and probably others of which we are ignorant, led to a general withdrawal of population from many areas and a concentration in the central portion of the Plateau.

THE REGRESSIVE AND HISTORIC-PUEBLO PERIODS

The period which followed the Great-Pueblo era and which lasted until historic times was called *Pueblo IV* under the Pecos Classification. It was defined as "the stage characterized by contraction of area occupied; by the gradual disappearance of corrugated wares; and, in general, by decline from the preceding cultural peak." [74] At the present time it is often referred to as the *Regressive-Pueblo* period.[110] This term is not really satisfactory. Admittedly, the latter part of the thirteenth and the beginning of the fourteenth century was a period of great instability, migrations occurred, and centers of population shifted. Once the shift had been made, however, important new communities developed in the drainages of the Little Colorado and the Rio Grande, and a renaissance began. It seems entirely possible that the Pueblo people might have achieved another remarkably high cultural stage had it not been for the arrival of the Spaniards in 1540.

Even after Europeans arrived in the Southwest, the native culture was far from being completely submerged, and, while aboriginal progress was retarded, it was not entirely stopped. Since the first advent of white men in the Southwest until the present day, the Pueblos have fought what sometimes appears to be a losing battle against the encroachment of European, and later, of American culture. Actually the battle has not yet been entirely lost. We shall never know how the Pueblo people might have developed, and what heights they might have reached had they been left to their own devices. At least, though, they have not been entirely assimilated by the civilization which has engulfed them, and they have succeeded in retaining some of their old way of life.

It might seem that as soon as written records become available for a period it should be classed as historic rather than prehistoric. The Pueblo Indians, however, were sufficiently successful in withstanding outside influences that the terminal date for the Regressive-Pueblo period is usually given as 1700, and only the period from 1700 to the present is called the *Historic-Pueblo* period.

The trend during Regressive-Pueblo times was toward larger houses. In the Hopi area the early houses were characterized by fine masonry and covered about an acre of ground. Later they became much larger and, in some cases, covered from ten to twelve acres of ground. These houses were sometimes made up of long rows of buildings with plazas between them. Kivas were rectangular, with a niche at one end of the room containing a bench. The normal size was about ten or fourteen feet square. On the floor, which was usually paved with stones, are found loom blocks. These are sandstone blocks with depressions designed to hold poles on which the warp threads are wound. The finding of these loom blocks in prehistoric kivas is most interesting, for, among the Hopi even today, the weaving is done by the men in the kivas. The use of commercially woven fabrics for most clothing has naturally curtailed the practice of this craft, but ceremonial clothing and fine white blankets which serve as wedding robes are still woven in the kivas.

The early pottery was largely black-on-yellow, but some polychrome ware was made, and there was also plain cooking pottery and some corrugated. The latter became progressively less widely used, and later cooking ware is almost entirely plain. In some later sites some of the black-on-yellow ware is marked by a distinctive stippling technique as black paint was splattered over the yellow backgound. During the period from 1400 to 1625 some of the most beautiful pottery ever made in the Southwest was being produced in the Hopi country. This is a polychrome ware which bears exceptionally fine designs, which include geometric and life forms and particularly graceful patterns, applied in red and black paint on a yellow background. Over forty years ago, archaeologists were excavating ancient villages in the Hopi country and finding examples of this beautiful ware. A woman of the village of Walpi, named Nampeyo, was the wife of one of the workmen employed by the expedition. She was already a fine potter, and she recognized the great artistry represented by these ancient vessels. She began to use similar designs and continued to produce remarkably fine pottery for over thirty years, although, for much of that time, her sight was

Fig. 36—Cavate dwellings and talus houses at Bandelier National Monument, New Mexico. (Courtesy National Park Service.)

failing and eventually she became blind, and the final painting of the graceful vessels which she had shaped had to be entrusted to others. The influence of this talented woman can still be seen in the fine pottery made by Hopi women of the First Mesa.

In the Zuñi district houses and kivas were much like those of the Hopi country. Pottery in this area was largely decorated with glaze paints. These are vitreous mixtures obtained by the use of lead in the paint. Glaze paints were difficult to apply and had a tendency to run or settle in masses. As a result, designs were poor, but the use of glazes was confined to decorations and entire vessels were not covered.

In the Rio Grande drainage, people with an earlier Pueblo culture were just beginning to come together into large communities when this period began. Doubtless, the advent of people from other parts of the Plateau province did much to intensify this trend. As time went by, houses became larger and fewer in number. Tuff blocks and adobe were widely used in their construction and there was some use of *cavate* dwellings. These are rooms, excavated into the back walls of caves, which have porchlike chambers in front.

Two famous Regressive-Pueblo sites in this region, which are known to many tourists, are Puye,[62] on the Pajarito Plateau, and Tyuonyi in El Rito de los Frijoles.[60] Beams from Puye have yielded tree-ring dates ranging from 1507 to 1565. This settlement, perched on a huge mass of yellowish gray tuff, consists of two aggregations of buildings. Forming a quadrangle on top of the mesa, were four, terraced community houses built around a court. There were also houses built in and against the cliff walls, usually at the top of the talus slope. At Tyuoni, whose dates range between about 1423 and 1513, there is a great communal house which was, in part, two stories high and roughly circular in form. It was made of tuff blocks. Three small kivas were built in the center court or plaza. A few hundred yards to the east of the ruin lies a large kiva. For a little over a mile along the canyon wall were cave rooms dug into the cliff and rows of small houses built of tuff blocks. Some of the cave rooms had porchlike structures erected in front of them, but others did not.

The largest and strongest pueblo during this period was Pecos, which lay at the headwaters of the Pecos River in northern New Mexico.[73] The first buildings were erected shortly before 1300, and final abandonment did not come until 1838. Such a long record is, of course, of tremendous archaeological importance, and it is indeed fortunate that some of the most extensive and painstaking excavations

Fig. 37—Tyuonyi, Bandelier National Monument, New Mexico. (Courtesy National Park Service.)

ever undertaken in the Southwest were at this site. There was evidence of at least six distinct towns. Great masses of pottery have been excavated, with careful attention being paid to stratigraphy, and very detailed studies have been made.[75] [77] Well over a thousand skeletons have been obtained and given careful study.

Throughout the Rio Grande area, glazed wares were widely made. The earlier forms had glazed designs applied on red vessels. Later, light colored vessels were used. A series of six different types of glazed wares, which were chronologically sequent, have been identified. By 1540 decorations were very carelessly applied and glazed wares were not of a high quality. It was not, however, until the latter part of the seventeenth century that they disappeared altogether and were replaced by light colored vessels, with designs in dull red and black paint, much like those made by the many present-day Indians.

Fig. 38—Glazed ware from the Rio Grande area. Regressive-Pueblo period. (Courtesy School of American Research.)

In the northern Rio Grande area black-on-white pottery died out to a great extent and was largely replaced by what we know as Biscuit Ware.[90] This name is derived from the resemblance of this pottery to china in the "biscuit stage" of manufacture. Biscuit ware is a thick pottery with a soft crumbly paste tempered with volcanic tuff. The background is a light gray or tan, and somewhat coarse designs are applied in black paint. Corrugated culinary ware was replaced by plain black pottery.

In southeastern New Mexico, and extending into Texas, a distinctive ware made during this period is found. This has a brown slip.

Bowl exteriors are undecorated, but the interiors have designs applied in red and black. Associated with it, is a plain brick-red ware.

The story of the Spanish conquest of the Southwest, which was interrupted by a revolt of the Pueblos in 1680, is as dramatic a tale as history can produce. Although 1540 is the date usually given for the first meeting between the Pueblo Indians and the Spaniards, it was actually in 1539 that the first contact occurred. In that year a Franciscan monk, Fray Marcos de Niza, accompanied by a Moor named Esteban, started north from Mexico to investigate tales of large and

Fig. 39—Biscuit ware from the Rio Grande area. Regressive-Pueblo period. (Courtesy School of American Research.)

wealthy cities which were rumored to lie in that direction. Esteban went on ahead, and, reaching what is now New Mexico, was slain by the Indians. Fray Marcos did not dare to proceed, but caught a glimpse of one of the pueblos of Zuñi from a distance, and returned with tales of great cities.

In 1540 an expedition was organized under the leadership of Francisco Vasquez de Coronado to search for the fabulous "Seven Cities of Cibola" in the north. After a long and difficult journey the expedition reached Hawikuh, one of the Zuñi villages. The disappointment of the adventurers may well be imagined, for here was no city of gold, ready to yield its wealth to the invaders, but a community of simple farmers who, not only had no riches, but had little conception of the role that wealth could play in society. Later, Coronado moved his forces to Tiguex on the Rio Grande, another Pueblo town. Trouble soon developed, and the Indians were massacred. The Spaniards then moved on to the Pueblo of Pecos, and there followed an expedition into the Plains as the search continued for the fabulous and mythical golden cities. In 1542, Coronado and his men withdrew to New Spain, and the Pueblos were left in peace for forty years. After 1580, various expeditions entered the Pueblo domain, and in 1598 it became a part of the Spanish dominions. In 1609 the city of Santa Fe was founded.

From the beginning there was a clash between the two cultures. The Pueblos resisted as best they could, but they were no match for the more highly organized Spaniards with their superior weapons and their inestimable advantage of being mounted. The colonizers and missionaries who entered the country looked upon the Indians as a subject people; there were abuses and many excesses, and the Indians were shamefully exploited. Corn, the all-important staple of the Indians, was requisitioned, and Spanish horses trampled Pueblo corn fields. Every effort was made to break down the prevailing form of government. Missionaries were determined to destroy the old religion and make converts among the natives. The principle, that the end justifies the means, was developed in its most pernicious form. There were floggings and hangings, and Indians were sold into slavery. All in all, it is a disgraceful page in history. Even the most cursory glance at our own record of dealings with various Indian groups, however, suggests that we are hardly in a position to "cast the first stone." Under the circumstances, even the smallest pebble would be excessive.

The presence of the Spaniards had other far-reaching and disastrous effects on the Pueblos. They had no immunity to European diseases, and many died. Worst of all, however, was the increasing pressure of fierce nomadic tribes. Tribes, such as the Utes, the Commanches, the Navajos and the Apaches, had been something of a menace before, but, as they acquired horses, stolen from the Spaniards, their mobility was greatly increased, and they became a scourge, sweeping over the Southwest, killing, pillaging, and destroying.

In 1642, there was a mild revolt of the Pueblo Indians against the Spaniards in which the Governor of the territory was killed, but they were not well organized and the revolt was soon put down. It was not until 1680 that a successful revolt took place. This dramatic episode in Southwestern history has been called "the first American Revolution." The success of the undertaking was largely due to Popé, an old medicine man of the Pueblo of San Juan. When the Spaniards first appeared there were some seventy villages. By 1680 the number had been greatly reduced. Added to the difficulties imposed by the lack of a common language, was the separation of the Pueblos, not only as regards distance, but in another and more important sense. As has already been pointed out, each of the pueblos was essentially a separate city-state with its own government, and, to some extent, its own culture. Popé, however, succeeded in interesting the people of the scattered communities in the common cause. First, the people of Taos were enlisted and then, one by one the other pueblos were added to the list, until all were united, including even the far off and peaceful Hopi.

At last, all was in readiness and a knotted cord was sent throughout the Pueblo domain, each knot representing one day which was to elapse before the warriors were to arise and cast out the invaders. Somehow the Spaniards learned of the plot, and the revolt took place a little earlier than had been planned. None the less, some four hundred people were killed, and the survivors fled to the garrison at Santa Fe. Santa Fe continued under siege until supplies and water were exhausted. When the town could no longer be held, troops and civilians marched away, without opposition from the Indians, and took refuge in the vicinity of what is now the city of El Paso, Texas.

For twelve years the Spaniards were kept out of the Pueblo country, although various attempts were made to retake the area. Even with the removal of the hated Spaniards, these were not happy times for the Pueblos. Mounted nomads as well as Spanish troops were a constant threat, and many groups were forced to move to mesa tops where defense was somewhat easier. As if all this were not enough, there came a severe drought which, to such people, can mean only suffering and starvation. At last in 1692, the land of the Pueblos again became a part of the Spanish domain. This time the conquest was bloodless. Don Diego de Vargas accomplished this remarkable feat largely by a display of force, coupled with a policy of turning the suspicions of the Pueblos against each other. United they had been able to drive out the invaders; divided they were powerless to prevent their return. It is a story to ponder carefully in these times.

Some Indians refused to accept Spanish domination and moved to the almost inaccessible Governador country of northern New Mexico where they lived among their traditional enemies, the Navajo, for some fifty years. Many Pueblo traits which appear in Navajo culture may stem from this contact. Other refugees joined the Hopis who were never reconquered. The reconquest did not by any means mark the end of

Fig. 40—Hopi maiden. Similar hair dresses are shown on figures in
Developmental-Pueblo pictographs and on Mimbres pottery.
(Courtesy Museum of Northern Arizona.)

all trouble. There continued to be periodic uprisings in the Rio Grande area, and the Spaniards did not have an easy time. In addition to their troubles with the Indians of the Pueblos, there was a constant threat from various wild predatory tribes. There was also much internal dissension as a result of a conflict between church and state. In 1821 the Pueblo homeland became part of the Republic of Mexico, and then, in 1848, New Mexico became a territory of the United States.

Throughout the period from 1540 until the present day, the Pueblos have been subjected to the influences of alien cultures. Some traits of these cultures they have accepted, others they have rejected. They have learned to keep livestock, they cultivate many fruits and vegetables unknown to their ancestors, they use metal tools and machinery. Machine-made fabrics are widely used, and there is an ever increasing trend toward wearing the white man's apparel. Pottery is still made, and interesting new wares have been developed, but it is made to be sold and, in Indian homes, most of the beautiful old vessels have been replaced by metal and china containers.

Nominally the people of the Pueblos are Christians, and there is no village without a chapel in which the people worship. There are kivas too, however, and sometimes openly, sometimes secretly, the old rites are practiced and the old gods are worshiped. Houses may have windows and galvanized roofs, but basically the architecture is the same. There is some dissension in various villages, but in many there is still a remarkable group unity. On the surface, there is an ever growing tendency for the Pueblo Indians to become more like the white neighbors who surround them, but it would be naive to believe that the old culture has disappeared completely. Perhaps some day it will, but the end is not yet. Those who know and understand the way of the "ancient ones" admit the inevitability of change, but they feel that there is much to be learned from the old way of life.

CHAPTER IV

THE HOHOKAM CULTURE

While the inhabitants of the Plateau were developing the culture described in the previous section, other groups in other parts of the Southwest were evolving along somewhat different lines. The next basic culture to be considered is that of the Hohokam, the people of the Desert Province whose center lies in the Middle Gila Basin and which includes the drainages of the Salt and Gila Rivers of southern Arizona.

Hohokam is a Pima word which means "those who have vanished." The ancient agriculturists, to whom this name has been given, lived in this semi-arid land for many centuries, and, through the use of canals, made a remarkable adjustment to an unfavorable environment. For a long time it was thought that they represented a regional variation of the Pueblo pattern, for the more spectacular ruins contained great communal houses of Pueblolike construction. Associated with these were small crude houses of wattle and daub construction. The large Pueblo houses were thought by some archaeologists to be temples or palaces, and the small houses were believed to be the homes of serfs or peons. When it was noted that different kinds of pottery were associated with the different types of houses, it became apparent that the situation was more complex than had been thought. Archaeological excavations finally brought the true explanation to light. During the first part of the fourteenth century, Pueblo people moved into the homeland of the Hohokam, bringing with them the techniques and traditions of their own culture which differed in many respects from those of the original inhabitants. The two groups lived together, but, to a great extent, each preserved the elements of its own culture.

There were certain similarities between the culture of the Hohokam and that of the Pueblos, but there were many differences. Both were agricultural people, but they used different types of corn and beans,[12] and there were certain differences in their farming techniques. Pottery was widely made in both societies but there were marked differences in manufacturing techniques and in color. Architectural development was entirely different. There were many differences in minor arts; for example, shell work was very highly developed among the Hohokam, and bone was used for tools much less than by the Pueblos. Probably there were physical differences between the two people, but our information on this subject is very scanty, for the Hohokam did not bury their dead, as did the Anasazi, but practiced cremation.

There is a strong possibility that the Hohokam developed from
the ancient food-gathering culture, known as the *Cochise,* which had
flourished in this same general region for many centuries.[54] The possibility has also been mentioned that the Hohokam may have come to

Fig. 41—Map of the Southwest showing sites referred to in Chapter IV.

1. Casa Grande	4. Roosevelt 9:6
2. Grewe Site	5. Snaketown
3. Los Muertos	6. Tonto National Monument

southern Arizona from the east with an already established pattern.[27]
Of course, the culture continued to evolve, but almost all of the basic
traits which characterize it were present in the earliest times of which
we have any record.

The question of dates for the Hohokam is, unfortunately, far more
complicated than in the case of the Basketmakers and Pueblos. The
wood available for house construction was usually cottonwood or mes-

quite, woods which are not suitable for tree-ring dating. Through strat-igraphic studies it has been possible to find the chronological place of various phases in relation to each other, but the establishment of an absolute chronology in terms of the Christian calendar is quite difficult, since it must be based almost entirely on cross-checking of pottery be-tween Hohokam and Anasazi sites. There is a considerable divergence between the dates suggested by different archaeologists, or even by the same archaeologist at different times. There is nothing to criticize in the fact that an archaeologist may give one date at one time and an entirely different one at another. Archaeologists, like all scientists, are seeking for the truth, and as new evidence is uncovered old estimates must often be changed and new ones made. First estimates placed the beginning of the culture in Arizona at about 300 B. C.[27] Later this date was revised upward by 900 years.[28] According to the most recent publication on the Hohokam, which contains approximate dates which will be used throughout the following discussion, this culture in the Gila Basin is believed to date back to about the beginning of the Christian era.[57]

There were several stages of development in the Hohokam, just as there were in the Anasazi culture with its six principal stages, ranging from Basketmaker to Historic-Pueblo times. The first is known as the *Pioneer* for this was the formative stage of the culture. The *Colonial* period which followed was, as the name implies, one in which colonies were established. During the next period, to which the name *Sedentary* has been given, the culture was fully developed. The term *Classic*, which is applied to the following period, is really a misnomer, for the cultural peak of the Hohokam had passed. It was, however, a time of high cultural development during which Pueblo and Hohokam people lived side by side in the Desert Province. Little is known of the Hohokam following the end of the Classic period when, about 1400 A. D., the Pueblo people moved away, but it is possible that the present Pima Indians may be descendants of the ancient Hohokam or that at least some Hohokam blood flows in their veins. A people with a variant form of the Hohokam culture who lived farther south may have been the forerunners of the present Papago Indians.

THE PIONEER HOHOKAM

The Pioneer period, according to recent estimates, began about the time of Christ and lasted for some five or six hundred years. It is possible, however, that these dates may have to be revised again, as more information becomes available. At present, unfortunately, this earliest period is known from only one site. This is a large site, called Snaketown,[27][28][31] which lies in the Gila Indian Reservation twelve miles southwest of Chandler, Arizona. It was occupied from Pioneer until Sedentary times, and has yielded a tremendous amount of information. It is extremely fortunate that this important site has been excavated with exceptional care and has been splendidly reported upon.

The Snaketown area is more arid than most other places occupied in prehistoric times and contains a stream that is now only intermittent, although it was probably perennial during the prehistoric period. Lumbering in the mountains and overgrazing have doubtless contributed materially to the desiccation of the region, but even in prehistoric times it must have been extremely dry. There is no evidence of the construction of irrigation canals which were so characteristic of later phases, but it seems possible that they may have existed at this time, although in a less well developed form, for without irrigation it would have been almost impossible for prosperous villages to arise in such a poor environment. Little is known, however, of the agricultural attainments of the people at this time. In fact, no corn has yet been found which may be attributed to this period, although it is certainly reasonable to suppose that it was being cultivated. The scarcity of bones of food animals indicates that meat did not play a very important part in the diet. Turkey bones are extremely rare. It is believed that turkeys were never domesticated by the Hohokam.

All Hohokam houses were earth lodges with much the same general plan. They were single-unit structures, usually with depressed floors. Entrance was through a covered passage or vestibule, normally in the middle of one side. Walls were constructed of poles, brush, and mud. The roofs, which consisted of rafters overlaid by smaller timbers, were supported by upright posts set in the floor. During Pioneer times houses were larger than in any other Hohokam period and in some cases were up to thirty-five feet square. Some archaeologists believe that the largest houses may have been occupied by more than one family.[31c] Others feel that it is more probable that they were ceremonial structures.[30] During most of the time, four or five roof supports were employed, but there was one phase early in the period when a great many posts set in rows were used and it is hard to see how such a house could have been lived in at all. So much skill was required to erect these houses that they certainly must not represent the people's first attempt at housebuilding, and there was undoubtedly an earlier phase for which evidence has not yet been found.

No material has been found which may be attributed to a pre-ceramic period, unless the Cochise culture proves to be ancestral to the Hohokam. Pottery is found in even the earliest Pioneer levels. The Hohokam did not have any corrugated pottery. All their wares were smooth and were produced by the paddle-and-anvil technique. When this method is used to shape and finish a piece of pottery, a round or mushroom-shaped object, known as an anvil, is held inside the vessel to receive the force of the blow, while the exterior is struck with a wooden paddle. Air was permitted to flow over the pottery while it was being fired, producing an oxidizing atmosphere.

There are important differences between the pottery making methods of the Hohokam and those of the Anasazi. As has been pre-viously noted, among the Anasazi, the final step in the finishing process was to shape and smooth the vessel through scraping with a gourd or pottery spoon, and most pottery was fired in a reducing atmosphere.

The earliest Hohokam pottery found is simple but well made. At first only plain undecorated wares in gray, brown, or red were produced. The temper contained flecks of mica which show through the surface. Bowls were usually red. Jars, which had a capacity of about two gallons, were normally gray or brown. Before long, painted decorations began to be applied. Designs were simple rectilinear or curvilinear forms. Hatching was widely used. Decoration was in a maroon-red paint on a grayish background, and the red portion was sometimes polished. As time went by, the background became a buff color rather than a gray. Because of this distinctive color combination, the term *Red-on-Buff* Culture was originally applied to the Hohokam.[32] During Pioneer times, some polychrome ware was made and it is believed that this may mark the first appearance of the use of multiple colors in the Southwest. This pottery has red and yellow designs on a gray back-ground. In many cases grooves were incised on bowl exteriors before the paint was applied. Even after painted pottery was introduced, it never made up more than twenty per cent of the total pottery of the Pioneer era.

Figurines, depicting human beings, as well as bowls and jars, were made of clay. These are known from the earliest times. They are quite similar to those of the Mexican Plateau, and it is thought that they may have been introduced from there, together with the knowledge of the cultivation of corn. These figurines have ridgelike noses pinched up from the base, and eyes and mouths represented by slits and dots. These were always modelled rather than made in molds. Some have funnel-shaped heads and may have served as containers. Figurines were usually fired, but this was not invariably the case.

Even from the earliest times the Hohokam appear to have cremated the dead, a practice which anthropologists always deprecate. These ancient people could hardly know how much they would inconvenience certain men in the twentieth century by their funerary habits, and

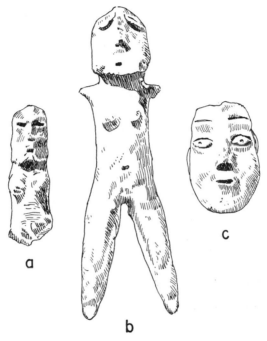

Fig. 42—Hohokam figurines. a. Pioneer period.
b. Colonial Period. c. Sedentary Period.

undoubtedly they would not have cared. Bones and ashes are rarely found in the Pioneer period but some have been recovered from pits and trenches. The actual cremation is not believed to have taken place here. There were offerings of crushed burned pottery, and late in the period some stone objects were used.

From the earliest times the Hohokam were skilled workers in stone. Two distinctive traits were: the manufacture of "palettes" and of stone jars. The palettes have been so called, although we are not sure of their actual function, because the center portions contain traces of ground pigment and there is usually a slight depression which might have resulted from grinding and mixing. They are the most common of Hohokam funerary offerings. In Pioneer times, they were much simpler than in later periods. At first they were plain stone slabs, but, by the close of the period, they were being made with raised borders. The polished stone vessels were sometimes plain, sometimes incised, and in one case the incisions had been filled with paint. Late in the period carved life-forms appeared. One effigy represents the figure of a man squatting and holding a shallow basin. Other stone implements include manos and metates, mortars and pestles, and highly polished grooved axes with raised ridges on either side of the groove. As has been previously noted, there was a scarcity of projectile points. Most of those which have been found are light enough to suggest the possibility of the use of the bow and arrow. There are also some heavy, stemmed points which may have been dart-points or knives.

Some stone was used in the manufacture of ornaments, although shell was more abundantly utilized for this purpose. Beads and pendants were carved from stone, and there was some use of turquoise, particularly in mosaic work. No ear plugs have been found in levels earlier than those of the Sedentary period, but they are shown on Pioneer figurines, and it seems reasonable to suppose that they may have been worn at that time. Shells provided many ornaments. Whole shells were utilized as beads by grinding off the ends to make it possible to string them; some disc beads were made. Bracelets were made of shell. They were usually thin and rather fragile and were not carved until late in the period.

Bone was much less widely used by the Hohokam than by the Anasazi, but one distinctive type of object was made of this material. This is an incised bone tube, usually decorated with rectilinear designs but sometimes utilizing curvilinear patterns and occasionally life-torms. There are some indications that these tubes were painted. Their use has not been determined.

Pipes were not made by the Hohokam in any period. Since these people were not as dependent on the vagaries of the weather as were the Anasazi, who depended to a great extent on flood irrigation, it is entirely logical that cloud symbols should not have been as important to them.

THE COLONIAL HOHOKAM

The Colonial period, which lasted from perhaps 600 to about 900 A. D., is better known than the Pioneer, for it is represented at two other excavated sites in addition to Snaketown. These are Roosevelt

9:6, at Roosevelt Lake, Arizona,[48] and the Grewe Site which lies just east of Casa Grande National Monument.[129] By the end of Colonial times all of the distinctive traits which characterize the Hohokam were fully developed, and some had even begun to decline. The most spectacular accomplishment of this period, and for that matter of the whole culture, was the construction of a great system of irrigation channels which diverted water to the fields from the rivers.[57] At their first appearance, the canals were so well developed that it seems impossible that this marks the first attempt at such a project. Possibly the system had been developed in Pioneer times, or, perhaps, it had been perfected elsewhere first, but evidence to bolster either theory is still lacking. By 700 A. D., the canal system was well established and became increasingly bigger and more complex until the peak was reached between 1200 and 1400 A. D.

The whole project is really amazing when one considers the tremendous amount of work which went into the construction and maintenance of the canals. The latter must have required almost as much effort as the original excavating, for silt was constantly being deposited. Canals were up to thirty feet wide and ten feet deep, and in the Salt River Valley they have been found to have an aggregate length of 150 miles. It staggers the imagination when one stops to think that this tremendous engineering feat was carried out with only the crudest of stone and wooden tools. The scope of such a project and the end toward which so much effort was directed tell us a great deal about the people who planned it. Undoubtedly such an undertaking indicates strong leadership and careful organization. Great numbers of people must have participated, and it undoubtedly took much careful planning to direct their labors. There must also have been some centralization of authority, since the canals served various settlements and these groups must have had some organization to direct their efforts toward the common good.

Here, as among the Anasazi, however, there is no evidence of a ruling class with a higher standard of living than that of their subordinates. The scope of the canal project suggests comparisons with the erection of the huge pyramids of Egypt or the great temples of the Maya. There is a tremendous difference, however, in the ends toward which all this vast human effort was directed. In Egypt, men slaved to construct tombs for despotic rulers, and, in the land of the Maya, they labored to erect temples, doubtless for the greater glory of the priesthood as much as for the gods who were worshipped. In

Fig. 43—Above, Hohokam house of the Colonial period. Below, large
ball court at Snaketown, Colonial period. (Courtesy Gila Pueblo.)

the arid reaches of the Hohokam homeland, however, the canals, which were built and kept open with so much labor, were for the benefit of the people.

The homes of the people continued to be simple structures consisting of single units. They were much like those of the Pioneer period but were smaller and rectangular with rounded corners. Usually they were constructed over a shallow pit, but some had elevated floors supported by stones. A fire pit lay in the floor just in front of the entrance. It is not known whether there were smoke holes or not. Walls were formed of slanting poles, and the interiors were lined with reeds. The roof rested on a central ridge pole supported by two main posts. There is evidence of outside kitchens, small brush structures containing a fire pit, much like those still used by the Pimas.

Houses and kitchens were not the only structures which were erected at this time, for ball courts made their first appearance during this period. These were large unroofed, oval areas, oriented east and west, and open at both ends. They were up to two hundred feet in length and were surrounded by walls believed to have been between fifteen and twenty feet in height and possibly higher. The earth banks, which formed the walls, sloped and were about twenty degrees off the perpendicular. The floor, which was well below ground level, was formed from smooth caliche deposits. Two stones set in the ends and one in the center apparently served as markers. They were very accurately placed and the one in the middle lies in the exact center. These are very much like the ball courts of the Maya, except that the latter had stone walls. There are a number of theories as to where these courts first originated. They may have been developed by the Maya and copied by the Hohokam, or they may have reached the Maya from the Hohokam. A third possibility is that both people received the idea from some still unknown source.

There is no way of knowing just what game was played by the Hohokam, but it is reasonable to suppose that it was much like that played in the courts farther south, and we know something of the rules from ancient manuscripts. The game was played with one, two, or more players on each side. The object was to knock a ball through rings set in the walls. Hands and feet could not be used, and the ball could be struck only with the knees, thighs, or buttocks. No rings have been found in the Hohokam courts, but it is probable that they would have been made of wood or some other perishable material, since the earth walls would hardly support great stone rings such as are found in some of the Mayan courts. It is quite possible that the game was connected with religious rites, as it was among the Maya.

Much red-on-buff and plain brown or buff pottery was manufactured. Most of the decorated vessels have designs formed by the repetition of small elements. These are often enclosed by small circles, and there was also a wide use of borders or fringes of short, oblique, parallel lines. The small elements included both geometric and life forms. There was a marked transition from the more rigidly formalized designs of the Pioneer period to the freer designs of later times. The practice of incising pottery declined and finally disappeared altogether. Firing clouds, which result when vessels come in contact with fuel while being fired, are quite common, and give the pottery a mottled appearance. Many figurines were made. They almost always depicted females. Early in the period they were made all in one piece, but later the head and body were made separately. The heads became more true to life. Clothing, leg and ankle bands, and, sometimes the eyes, were indicated by appliqué.

Pottery and figurines served as offerings for the dead. Small

Fig. 44—Red-on-buff Hohokam vessel of the Colonial period.
(Courtesy Gila Pueblo.)

sherds were still common, but whole vessels also began to be used. There were three types of cremations. Sometimes bones, ashes, and offerings are found in pits dug into the caliche and it appears probable that the actual burning took place there. In other cases they are found in trenches. Sometimes burning took place elsewhere and later the burned remains were placed in small holes close together. In addition to objects made of clay, stone projectile points and palettes are usually found in the cremations.

Palettes, which were the most consistent offering, were made of thin schistose rock. There is a clear differentiation between the center portion and the border which is ornamented with grooves. Some have sculptured edges in the form of birds, snakes, and other animals. There are also effigy types in which the outline of the palette is in a life-form. Palettes were most numerous early in the Colonial period and later declined in importance. One extremely interesting feature of many of these objects is that on the mixing surface of heavily burned palettes from cremations is found a vitreous substance which, on analysis, proved to be a lead mixture. It is not certain whether the use of lead ore was intentional or accidental, but in any case the Hohokam never learned to exploit this as metal. It has been suggested that the change in the lead mixture from a dull color to a brilliant red with metallic globules may have been observed as the palettes burned on the funeral pyres and that it came to have a ceremonial significance. It is entirely possible, however, that the palettes had simply been used for grinding a compound containing lead, which was used to provide pigment, prior to the burning. They may have been used to mix facial or body paint.

Some of the most remarkable stone work found in Hohokam sites consisted of mosaic plaques or mirrors inlaid with angular pieces of iron pyrites which had a reflecting quality. These were common funerary offerings, and as a result most of the specimens obtained are badly damaged. None the less, one can still appreciate the amazing work which went into their construction. These plaques or mirrors range between three and eight inches in diameter. On one surface are thin sheets of iron pyrites crystals carefully fitted together. How these thin plates were obtained is a complete mystery, for pyrites crystals are usually cubic and so hard that they cannot be scratched with a knife. In some cases the crystal encrustation covered the entire face, in others edges were beveled. Edges and backs were sometimes decorated with something which resembles cloisonné work, although the technique differed. First a base coat of a gray material was applied, and then this was covered with a thicker layer of some black substance. A design was cut into this with a sharp implement, and then the sunken portion was half filled with thick white paint. Next, paint in a variety of colors was added to fill the depression, or, in some cases, was even built up slightly above the level of the black background portion.

These mirrors are almost exactly like those found in sites in Central America. It is thought that the best examples found in Hohokam sites were imported from the south,[59] although it is possible that some crude imitations may have been made by the Hohokam themselves. The material necessary would have been available to them, for sizeable pyrites crystals are found near Tucson.

Many stone vessels were made. They were usually carved in bas relief and both realistic and life-forms were used. Desert reptiles were the most common figures. Other objects made of stone included abraders for use in shell work, metates which were not very precisely shaped, a few stone finger-rings, and projectile points. These were long slender points which were barbed and serrated.

Fig. 45—Hohokam carved stone vessel of the Colonial period.
(Courtesy Arizona State Museum.)

Shell was very widely used. A few needles made of shell have been found, but this was apparently not considered a utilitarian material and it was most often used in the manufacture of ornaments. Shell beads and pendants continued to be used, and many bracelets

Fig. 46—Hohokam ornaments of carved shell. (Courtesy National Park Service.)

were made. These were made of Glycymeris shells which are nearly circular and, when cut in cross-section, provide a suitable arm band. Carving did not reach its peak until the following period, but fine bracelets were produced. Birds, snakes, frogs, and geometric forms furnished the designs. The most frequent motif is a bird-and-snake combination. The snake's head is in the bird's mouth and the body of the snake forms the band. This quite probably had some special ceremonial significance. Carved rings, which first appeared at this time, are usually in the form of snakes. They were never as abundant as bracelets. There was some mosaic work with shell, but this art did not fully develop until later. Birds and snakes, often in combination, were the usual subjects for carving on bone.

THE SEDENTARY HOHOKAM

During the Sedentary period, which lasted from about 900 to 1200 A. D. there was some withdrawal from the outlying districts and a greater concentration of population in a smaller area, although there was also some northward extension of the culture. There was some regional specialization during the latter part of the period, for the inhabitants of the upper or eastern portion of the Gila Basin developed somewhat differently from those of the central area. This was possibly the result of the influence of Pueblo people who lived in the Tonto Basin about one hundred miles to the northwest, and it presaged the changes which were to occur in the next period when some of these people moved into the Hohokam area, bringing with them their distinctive culture.

Houses in the main area were roughly rectangular in outline, but the ends were somewhat rounded and the sides slightly convex. Floors were encircled by low, mud rims, six inches or less in height, which were probably designed to keep water out of the houses. Some had parallel-sided entrance ways, but others had a bulbous vestibule with a low step at the end. Late in the period, in the eastern part of the Gila Basin, there were some rectangular surface houses with walls of adobe, containing sporadic stones, over a pole framework. In some cases, villages were enclosed by walls and are referred to as *compounds*. This name is taken from the term which is applied to the walled or fenced enclosure of a house or factory in the orient.

The irrigation system was enlarged and improved. Ball courts were still being built but they seem to have been considerably reduced in size by the end of the period. They were oriented north and south and the ends were closed. One interesting find, made in a Sedentary site with an estimated date of 1100 A. D., was a rubber ball buried in a jar.[52] Analysis showed the rubber to be of American origin, unvulcanized and unrefined. There is no way of proving that this ball was used in playing the game for which the courts were designed, but it seems entirely possible that it was.

At this time some Hohokam people moved north into the Flagstaff area. They introduced ball courts and other distinctive traits of their culture.[86]

Fig. 47—Red-on-buff Hohokam jars of the Sedentary period.
(Courtesy Gila Pueblo.)

In the field of pottery, forty per cent of all that was produced was of the red-on-buff variety. There was a great elaboration of designs and some appear to have been taken from woven fabrics. Panels, negative designs, and patterns tied together by interlocking scrolls, were all common. There was a great variety of shapes which included three and four-legged trays. Jars increased tremendously in size, and a few had a capacity of almost thirty gallons. Bowls were also quite large. Some plain buff ware was manufactured, but it was not common. Less than one per cent of the total pottery assemblage consisted of bowls with heavily slipped and polished reddish brown interiors and mottled brown or gray exteriors. From the eastern area come bright red bowls with smoke-darkened, black interiors.

Figurines were of two types. For the most part they consisted of heads which were apparently attached to bodies made of cord-wrapped fiber. These have not survived, but their presence is indicated by impressions in the clay of the heads. The faces are quite realistic and probably represent an attempt at portraiture. Other figurines, made of buff clay and painted with red, show full figures, seated, with hands resting on the knees.

It is most unfortunate that practically none of the textiles produced at this time have lasted through the centuries. A few fragments have been found which give us tantalizing glimpses of a highly developed craft. Apparently very fine cotton textiles with intricate weaves were produced. No baskets have survived the passage of the years, but ash casts have been found which show that the making of baskets was well developed.

Cremation was still the accepted method of disposing of the dead, although a few burials have been found. Apparently inhumation was tried on a very small scale, but it did not supplant cremation. Bodies and offerings were usually burned, and then the unconsumed portions gathered together and put in small pits dug in the caliche. In some cases, bodies and offerings were left in the pit in which they were burned, and the pit covered with earth. In the eastern part of the Gila Basin, unconsumed bones and offerings were placed in small pottery urns and buried with a small bowl or sherd covering the mouth of the urn.

Mosaic plaques or mirrors were still used. Palettes continued to serve as mortuary offerings, but they had decreased in number and had greatly degenerated. Raised borders disappeared and only incised lines remained to differentiate the rim and the mixing surface. Some palettes have been found in the area around Flagstaff in a site dated

Fig. 48—Hohokam stone palette of the Sedentary period.
(Courtesy Arizona State Museum)

as late as 1278, so the trait seems to have persisted in the north longer than in the Hohokam province where it appears to have originated.

Stone vessels continued to be made, but they too were decadent. Carving in relief was largely replaced by incising. Life-forms in relief, when they do appear, are highly conventionalized. Many of the vessels are of steatite. There were some effigy vessels, representing animals and birds, which had shallow basins hollowed out of the backs. Metates and mortars and pestles were well shaped. Some hoes first appeared during Sedentary times, and it is thought that they may have been intrusive. Stone projectile points were long and slender and beautifully flaked. About half had lateral notches and the others were unnotched forms characterized by deep serrations. Stone was widely used as a material for ornaments. A great variety of disc beads were manufactured and the first ear plugs are found in sites of this period, although, as has been previously noted, they are seen on Pioneer figurines and quite possibly had been worn since the earliest times. Some particularly interesting finds include stone objects believed to have been nose-buttons or labrets. Figurines do not show the use of nose-buttons, but they do show ornaments just below the corners of the mouth and these may have been worn through the fleshy part of the chin. Ornaments worn through the nose or chin strike us as strange, for they have never won approval in our particular society, but they have been quite common in other parts of the world. In any case, a glimpse at a woman's hat shop today offers convincing proof that anything can become fashionable and socially acceptable.

Shell work, already so well developed among the Hohokam, reached its peak in Sedentary times. Mosaic work, in which both shell and turquoise were used, achieved its highest development. The technique employed must be described as overlaying, rather than as inlaying, for depressions were not cut to receive the pieces which, instead, were laid on the surface. Due to the placing of these mosaics in the cremation fires, we know little of their composition beyond the fact that shell was usually used to provide a base for the overlay. Individual pieces were cut in the forms of animals or geometric figures. Disc beads, characterized by large perforations, and pendants were widely made. For the latter, the trend was away from life-forms and toward geometric figures. Many finely carved bracelets were made. Shells with painted designs appear first in Sedentary levels, but, due to the impermanent nature of the paint, there is no assurance that this technique may not have been developed some time before.

The most interesting treatment of shells is exemplified by those with designs applied by an etching process. The Hohokam may have been the first people to discover the technique of etching, for they were using it about the eleventh or twelfth century and the earliest recorded use of the process is on a coat of armor made in Europe in the 15th century.[57] Among the Hohokam the process does not appear to have continued beyond Sedentary times. It was probably never very commonly used and the difficulty of controlling the medium may have contributed to an early abandonment. Painting and etching were sometimes combined, for an example has been found of a shell etched with geometric designs and painted with red and green pigment.

Fig. 49—Hohokam etched shell. Sedentary period.
(Courtesy Arizona State Museum)

Since shell is nearly pure calcium carbonate it is easy to see why portions exposed to the action of acid would be eaten away, but we have no way of being sure exactly what the technique used may have been.

Experiments conducted in the laboratories of Gila Pueblo, however, have shown how such results could have been obtained with available materials.[31] The problem of finding a suitable acid was first considered. Obviously, for the ancient Hohokam, the problem could not be solved by running down to the corner drugstore. For the purposes of the experiment, a mild acetic acid solution was produced by fermenting juice from the fruit of the giant cactus. Portions of a shell were covered with pitch, a material which resists acid, and the shell immersed in the acid for seventy-two hours. When it was removed, the pitch-covered portion stood out in relief while the exposed parts had been partially eaten away, duplicating the effect found on the prehistoric shells.

Bone tubes continued to be made, but they were plain and undecorated. Other bone artifacts include daggerlike objects with carved heads, which may have served as hair ornaments. Usually the carving represented the heads of mountain sheep or a bird-and-serpent motif.

It was in the Sedentary level at Snaketown that the first objects made of metal were found. These were little copper bells, pear-shaped and split at the bottom, which very much resemble sleigh-bells. A great many identical bells are found in Mexico and it seems probable that the Snaketown examples were imported from there.[59] In the Anasazi area many copper bells were imported from the south. Most of them are dated at between 1300 and 1400 A. D., although some have been found which were brought into Pueblo Bonito and Aztec at an earlier date.

THE CLASSIC HOHOKAM

The Classic period of the Hohokam, which lasted from about 1200 to 1400 A. D. or not long thereafter, was a remarkable era which has been referred to as "the Golden Age of southern Arizona". As has been previously noted, however, *Classic* is hardly an accurate designation since we are no longer dealing with a pure Hohokam culture. It was during this time that Pueblo traits and, later, Pueblo people themselves entered the Hohokam homeland.

The newcomers, whose influence had been felt even before they themselves arrived, were a group known as the Salado people. The Saladoans are believed to have originated in the Little Colorado area, which they left to move farther south into the Tonto Basin around 1100 A. D.[56] About 1300 they again moved farther south and entered the domain of the Hohokam. They brought with them their own distinctive culture which differed in some ways from the classic Pueblo of the San Juan area and was far different from that of the Hohokam. They built thick-walled, multi-storied communal houses of adobe, in walled compounds. Their pottery included coiled and scraped polychrome wares in red, black, and white. They practiced inhumation, or burial of the dead.

Fig. 50—Salado polychrome ware.
(Courtesy National Park Service.)

The coming together of the Salado people and the Hohokam is really remarkable. There is no evidence of an invasion nor of violence. Instead, these two culturally different people seem to have come together in a friendly manner and lived together in the same communities in peace and amity. Each group, to a great extent, clung to its own way of life, yet together they achieved a distinctive culture. It was during this period that the canal system reached its highest development. Doubtless the newcomers, who had had no real irrigation system before, contributed their labor to the common project of building and maintaining the canals which were built to serve their villages.

In the Hohokam culture proper there were certain changes. Pottery included plain buff ware and a pebble-polished bright red ware, usually in the form of bowls with black interiors, as well as the ubiquitous red-on-buff. In the latter, the red paint was thinner and less brilliantly colored than in earlier times. Jars and pitchers, the latter an innovation of this period, were the commonest forms. Jars with a capacity of over thirty gallons have been found. Painting was characterized by poor brush work. Most designs were rectilinear and practically no life-forms were used. A few figurines, representing both human beings and animals, have been found at Los Muertos, a Classic site, but they were too few to have been important in the culture. There is, of course, the possibility that some were made of perishable materials instead of clay and hence have not survived.

Most Salado pottery during this period was a polychrome ware with red, black, and white. Red was sometimes used as a decorative color, and sometimes formed a part of the background. Bowls and jars predominated, but ladles and mugs were also made, and there were some effigy vessels, usually in the form of birds. Some corrugated pottery was also made.

There was a definite decline in some of the arts of the Hohokam. Carved stone vessels and palettes were no longer made. Pyrites mirrors are not found in this horizon. Shell work continued to flourish, although etching had disappeared. Heavy bracelets were made and true inlay and ceremonial shell trumpets [5] made their first appearance. These were west-coast conch shells with a hole ground into the tip of the spire. Blowing into the shell through this hole produces a trumpetlike sound.

Axes, both single and doublebitted, were beautifully made, and represented stone work at its peak. Projectile points were thin and well made. Uusually they were long and triangular. Most of them had notches chipped at right angles but a few were unnotched. Edges were not serrated, as they had been in earlier times. Stone implements, presumably of Salado origin, were added to the complex. These included adzes, picks, chisels, crushers, club heads, flakes with serrated edges which served as saws, jar stoppers, pottery scrapers, and shaft straighteners.

Ball courts were greatly reduced in size by Classic times and it seems probable that the game played in them had lost much of its popularity. This belief is confirmed by the absence of a ball court at Los Muertos, one of the largest and most important villages. It seems likely that provisions would have been made at such a settlement for a sport which enjoyed much popular support. A ball court was found at Casa Grande, another important Classic site, however, so this trait had apparently not disappeared entirely.

It was in the realm of architecture that the greatest changes occurred. Even in Sedentary times, in the eastern part of the Hohokam area, there was a tendency for houses to become surface structures. During the early part of the Classic period, surface houses, sometimes with contiguous rooms, were built by the Hohokam. These changes were probably due to Salado influence, although the people themselves had not yet arrived in the area. Walls were still extremely thin and of typical Hohokam construction, so houses were no more than one story high.

With the arrival of the Salado people, the building of multi-storied houses with massive walls, enclosed in compounds, began. Two of the best known of these are El Pueblo de Los Muertos. (The City of the Dead) [56] which, before its destruction by farmers, lay a few miles south of Tempe, Arizona, and Casa Grande,[26] a great ruin, now a National Monument, which lies nine miles west of Florence, Arizona.

Los Muertos covered a large area and contained thirty-six communal buildings and many small houses. It was a settlement which could not have existed without irrigation, and ditches have been traced which brought water to it from the Salt River. The largest single building was a great rectangular house enclosed on all four sides by a massive wall which reached a thickness of seven feet in some places. Some of the outer walls of the big house achieved a comparable thickness. In addition to the main structure, the compound contained plazas and small house clusters. Another ruin contained two large house clusters. Here some of the rooms had very thin walls, as do the Hohokam houses of Sedentary and early Classic times.

At Los Muertos the Hohokam and the Salado people apparently lived side by side, each clinging for the most part to their own traditions. This divergence was particularly marked in the disposal of the dead. The Saladoans usually buried their dead under house floors or in the plaza. The body was normally extended, with the head to the east. Pottery, jewelry, and some stone artifacts served as grave offerings. The Hohokam continued to practice cremation. The dead were placed on wooden gratings over shallow pits, and the grating was consumed with the body. The unconsumed bones and ashes were placed in jars and buried in special plots near the refuse heaps. There seems to have been some borrowing between the two groups, for occasionally inhumations are found accompanied by the red-on-buff pottery of the Hohokam, and a few cremations have been found with Salado offerings or in polychrome vessels. This borrowing, however, seems to have been

Fig. 51—Great House built by the Salado people. Casa Grande National Monument, Arizona. (Courtesy National Park Service.)

sufficiently limited to make it possible, on the basis of the numbers of burials and cremations, to estimate what the comparative ratio of Hohokam to Salado people may have been. On this basis, the Hohokam appear to have outnumbered the foreign element by a ratio of three to one.

The famous site of Casa Grande consists of a group of ruins made up of house clusters surrounded by compound walls. Both thin-walled, single-roomed houses and multiple-roomed structures with massive walls are represented. Of the latter, the outstanding example is a building known as the "Great House" which lies in an enclosure called Compound A. The Great House is four stories high, but only eleven rooms are represented. Originally there were five additional rooms on the ground floor, but these were filled in to form an artificial terrace. The rooms are arranged with one on the top floor and five rooms on each of the two lower stories. Some rooms were entered by small doors, and others through the roof. There were no windows. The walls of the Great House now stand some thirty-four feet above ground level and are over four feet thick. No forms were used, and the wall was constructed by a process of piling up layers of stiff caliche mud. Each course was patted into shape and then allowed to dry to receive the next course. The final finish was obtained by plastering with a thin mud mixture made with sieved caliche.

While the foregoing refers to the Hohokam who lived in the river valleys, there was another group who lived farther to the south in the desert region known as the Papagueria.[57] Here agriculture was more limited, for the only form of irrigation was by ditches designed to divert rain water to the fields. With a less favorable environment, the standard of living was lowered and the reduction of leisure time resulted in a poorer development of arts and crafts. Although the material culture was not as rich as in the more favored river valleys, any loss is more than compensated for, from the archaeological point of view, by the fact that the greater aridity of this region has made possible the preservation of much normally perishable material. The ancient desert dwellers further endeared themselves to archaeologists by forsaking cremation about the beginning of the eleventh century.

A remarkable site, known as *Ventana Cave*,[55] which lies in the Papago Indian Reservation, has yielded great quantities of very fine material, including some forty burials, and the final report of this valuable discovery is eagerly awaited. Preliminary reports indicate that the ancient inhabitants of this region strongly resembled the Papago Indians

Fig. 52—Child's cotton poncho from Ventana Cave. Desert Hohokam, eleventh or twelfth century. (Courtesy Arizona State Museum.)

who still occupy it. The early people were fine weavers and made cotton cloth which, together with rabbit-fur blankets and sandals, provided them with clothing.

One strong difference between the Hohokam of the river valleys and those of the desert area lies in the fact that the Salado people did not penetrate into the desert section and the culture of this region accordingly remained relatively untouched. This isolation seems to have been deliberately achieved by the desert dwellers who erected strings of forts of rough laid stone on volcanic hills to protect their domain. Environment may well have played a strong part in the reaction of the two groups of Hohokam to new people. With their meager resources the people of the Papagueria could hardly accept additions to the population, while the more prosperous group to the north, blessed with the water which means so much in the Southwest, could afford to be friendly.

THE RECENT HOHOKAM

About 1400 A. D., the Salado people left the Gila country. It is thought that some may have moved east as far as eastern New Mexico and southeast into Chihauhua. Others from the Upper Gila may have drifted north into the Zuñi area. We cannot be sure of the reason for their departure, but one theory, which has been advanced, is that they may have been forced out by the arrival of the Apaches.[27] What happened to the Hohokam themselves we do not know. Possibly they remained in the same district and eventually sites belonging to the period after 1400 may be found. It is also possible that they may have moved to the inhospitable reaches of the Papagueria which would have afforded greater protection against an enemy.

Although there is a gap in our information, the belief is widely held that the Hohokam may have been the ancestors of the present Pima Indians and possibly the Papago, related tribes who speak mutually intelligible dialects of the Piman language. The most convincing argument for this theory is that the Pimas were well established in the Gila Basin, the old Hohokam homeland, when they were discovered by the Spaniards in 1530. The Papago still occupy the desert region of the Papagueria. In general, the way of life of these people was not too different from that of the Hohokam. They were agriculturists, dependent on irrigation, lived in one-room houses, and their pottery was somewhat similar to that of the Hohokam. Quite possibly,

Fig. 53—Pima House in 1897. (Courtesy National Park Service.)

other racial strains are present and other groups contributed to the Pima and Papago culture, but it seems highly probable that the Hohokam was one of the most important elements.

SUMMARY

We may characterize the Hohokam as follows: They were a prehistoric agricultural people of southern Arizona who may have been the descendants of the western branch of the ancient food-gathering people of the Cochise Culture. They made an amazing adjustment to an unfavorable environment through the use of an extensive canal system. They lived in one-room houses of wattle-and-daub construction with depressed floors and covered side passages or vestibules. Some big houses built during the earliest period may have sheltered more than one family or they may have been ceremonial structures. There were large courts where it is thought that a ball game similar to that of the Maya was played.

Pottery was made by the paddle-and-anvil technique and fired in an oxidizing atmosphere. Undecorated plain ware was mostly buff, although ranging in shade from gray to brown. Decorated pottery usually had designs in red paint on a buff background. In an early period there was a rare polychrome ware which had red and yellow designs on a gray background. Figurines were also made of clay.

Stone work was well developed. Stone vessels, often with fine carving, were widely made. Well carved palettes are a distinctive trait of the culture. Mosaic plaques or mirrors, made of pyrites crystals, believed to have been imported from the south, were often used as funeral offerings.

Shell was widely used in the manufacture of ornaments, particularly bracelets. It was usually ornamented by carving, but in a few cases an etching technique was employed. Weaving was apparently well developed, but only a few specimens have been preserved, so our information on this point is scanty.

Disposal of the dead was by cremation. Funerary offerings were burned with the body, and included pottery, figurines, palettes and pyrites mirrors. Ashes, calcined bones, and offerings were gathered together after the cremation and buried. Burial was at first in trenches, later in pits or urns.

About 1300 A. D., Pueblo people moved into the Hohokam country and for the next hundred years the two groups lived together. There was some amalgamation of the two cultures, but in most important respects they remained distinct in spite of the closeness of the association. About 1400 A. D. the newcomers moved away. We have no clear information as to just what happened to the Hohokam after that time, but it is possible that they may have remained in the same general vicinity and have been the forerunners of the Pima and Papago Indians who occupied that territory at the time of the arrival of the Spaniards.

CHAPTER V

THE MOGOLLON CULTURE

Writing about the Mogollon Culture is rather like dealing with a time bomb. It is impossible to ignore it, but one has the uncomfortable feeling that whatever one does about it is likely to be wrong. In the relatively few years which have elapsed since it was first suggested that it was a separate entity [89] and not just a regional variation of the Basketmaker-Pueblo pattern, there have come to be many theories.[102] Many archaeologists are convinced that it must be given the status of a basic culture comparable to that given to the Anasazi and the Hohokam,[50][84] but there are some who feel that it should be regarded as a variant of the Anasazi, and others who consider it the result of an early fusion of Anasazi and Hohokam.[99] Unfortunately, too few sites have been excavated to evaluate fully all the conflicting theories. It has been said that "The Mogollon appears to be an illegitimate whose paternity is still under scrutiny."*

We do know that a group of people lived in west-central New Mexico and east-central Arizona who were largely contemporaneous with the Anasazi and the Hohokam and shared some traits with both cultures, particularly the former. At least during the earliest periods, however, they had a culture distinctive enough to cause many archaeologists to feel that it is impossible to equate them with any other group.

Although the origins of the Mogollon are still shrouded in mystery, one likely theory, which has been advanced by those who favor the belief that the Mogollon is a basic culture, is that the Mogollon people may be descendents of the eastern branch of the ancient food gatherers of the Cochise Culture.[54] Their stone work is similar, and, while the earliest Mogollon people did practice agriculture and hunting, they too seem to have had an economy based to a great extent on the gathering of wild plant foods. Apart from the problem of origins, there is the further consideration of determining to what extent the early Mogollon people were influenced by other people and to what extent they influenced others. This is one of the most important questions with which Southwestern archaeologists are struggling today.

Much further work will be necessary before even a partially satisfactory answer is found. For the present, there are a few facts and innumerable conjectures. In a publication of this nature, all that may be attempted is to outline the available factual material and indicate some of the theories to which it has given rise.

*Ref. 72, p. 433.

The name assigned to the culture was derived from the Mogollon range of mountains which lies in the district in which many of the chief ruins have been found. The principal sites which have been excavated lie in the valleys of the San Francisco and Mimbres rivers in

Fig. 54—Map of the Southwest showing sites referred to in Chapter V.

1. Bear Ruin
2. Cameron Creek Village
3. Galaz Ruin
4. Harris Village
5. Mattocks Ruin
6. Mogollon Village
7. Starkweather Ruin
8. SU site
9. Swarts Ruin

west-central New Mexico, in the Forestdale Valley of Arizona, and in southeastern Arizona. It is probable that, as further work is done, the geographical range of the culture may be further increased. The area in which Mogollon remains have already been found is a large one, equally as extensive as the Basketmaker. Proponents of the theory that the Mogollon is a basic culture point out that it is an important fact that it has geographic substance.[59]

It would be pleasant to be able to divide the Mogollon into clear-cut periods with established dates and full lists of the traits which characterize each stage. Unfortunately, this cannot be done. It has been possible to determine, in a general way, the stages of cultural development in certain sites in New Mexico where there was some degree of uniformity. In other areas, however, conditions were different, and it is impossible to say that at any given time all the Mogollon people had the identical type of culture, although there are enough points of similarity to permit us to assign them all to the same general group. It seems probable that, as further work is done, separate regional chronologies will be worked out as has been done for the Pueblo sequence where we recognize significant differences between cultural centers such as Chaco, Mesa Verde, and Kayenta.[59] For the present these regional variations add to the complexity of the problem. A further complication arises from the fact that even those who recognize the Mogollon as a basic culture feel that it is only during the earliest times that they are dealing with a relatively pure culture, and that after 700 or 800 A. D. the Mogollon Culture was beginning to be assimilated by the Anasazi, and that there were also Hohokam influences.

Dates for Mogollon sites are very difficult to determine, for only a few tree-ring dates are available. One find tends to suggest a considerable antiquity for the culture. At Snaketown, in the earliest Pioneer level, was found a polished red ware, which, through petrographic analysis, has been shown to contain materials not used at Snaketown, but identical with those of wares from Mogollon sites.[31 a] This pottery is better made than the early Hohokam pottery and would suggest that the Mogollon people had been making pottery for some time prior to the beginning of the Christian era. Another possibility which has been suggested is that both they and the Hohokam obtained pottery from some other source which has not yet been identified.[99]

BLUFF RUIN [58]

The earliest dendrochronologically dated Mogollon site yet found lies in the Forestdale Valley of Arizona. Tree-rings indicate that it was occupied about 300 A. D. As far as it is possible to judge on the basis of the very meager information available in publications at this time, the people who lived at this site, which is known as Bluff Ruin, had a very simple culture. They lived in round pit houses which were entered through the side. The little pottery which has been found is plain brown ware.

THE PINE LAWN PHASE [84] [85]

At present the Mogollon in New Mexico is divided into four periods. To the first has been assigned the name *Pine Lawn Phase*. It is known only from one location, the SU site which lies about seven miles west of Reserve, New Mexico. The site name was taken from a local cattle brand. No wood suitable for dating has been found, so it has been necessary to estimate the time of occupation on typological evidence. On this basis, it is thought that the SU site was inhabited prior to 500 A. D.

Most of the inhabitants of the SU site lived in very shallow pit houses. These were so irregular in shape, and there was such variation in size and construction, that it has been suggested that the indications are that house building was a relatively new trait. The greater number of the pit houses were entered by inclined passageways opening to the east. There were no deflectors such as are found in Basketmaker houses.

A few surface houses with wattle-and-daub walls have also been found. They are similarly irregular in shape and size. House floors, both in pit and surface structures, contained pits. There were usually several of these and in one case as many as eight. The largest were over three feet in diameter. Most were empty, and it is thought that they served as storage spaces, but a few contained burned stones and bones and may have been used for cooking. Few houses contained fire pits such as are normally found in Anasazi dwellings.

Pottery consisted of three undecorated wares which, like all early Mogollon pottery, were produced by a coiling and scraping technique and fired in an oxidizing atmosphere. Included are a burnished buff to reddish-brown ware, a thick unpolished brown, and a polished red. All were made of the same type of clay and this argues against the polished red pottery having been of foreign manufacture as has sometimes been suggested.

Stone and bone artifacts were not very carefully worked, and many materials seem to have been utilized without much modification. Stone tools and implements strongly resemble ancient Cochise specimens. Many grinding stones were found and quite a number of them were basin-shaped types such as were used in the preparation of wild plant foods. There were some simple paint-grinding stones. Little unworked bone was found and this bears out the theory that no great amount of hunting was done. Worked specimens were largely made from the long bones of deer. They include pinlike objects and awls. Some of the latter had notches cut in the side.

A total of forty-six burials has been uncovered. Some bodies were buried outside of the houses and some within the walls. These were usually flexed and most of them had been placed in pits. Only a few artifacts were found with the skeletons, and it appears that the practice of burying offerings with the dead was not well established. The skeletons were poorly preserved and have not yielded much information. Deformation of the skull was rare, and, when present, was very slight. It has been suggested that the poor condition of the bones, as compared with animal bones from the same site, may reflect deficiencies in the people's diet.

The succeeding periods have been found best represented at Mogollon Village,[50] about ten miles north of Glenwood, New Mexico; at Harris Village,[50] a quarter of a mile east of Mimbres, New Mexico; and at Starkweather Ruin,[99] three and a half miles west of Reserve, New Mexico.

The excavation of these sites has yielded evidence of occupation by prehistoric people who practiced agriculture but who were more dependent on hunting than their neighbors to the north and west. Corn was cultivated, but there is no evidence of beans or squash. They used the atlatl or dart-thrower, as well as the bow and arrow. There is no evidence that turkeys were domesticated, although bone remains indicate that they were hunted.

THE GEORGETOWN PHASE

The earliest period represented at these sites is known as the *Georgetown*. The estimated dates are from 500 to 700 A. D.[50] Some archaeologists do not agree, and feel that 700 A. D. is the earliest date which may be given for the first Mogollon settlements in New Mexico.[99] During Georgetown times dwellings were small, roughly circular, pit houses which were entered by inclined passageways. A fire pit lay midway between the center of the room and the entrance. Roofs were supported by a main pole in the center of the structure and secondary poles along the walls. One larger pit house was found at Harris Village which, it is thought, may have been used for ceremonial purposes. It did not contain the deflector, sipapu, or benches which characterize most Pueblo kivas. It differs from the Georgetown domiciliary structures not only in size but in the greater length of the entrance passage and the possession of a straight front wall.

Most pottery was undecorated. Only four sherds of painted pottery, which consisted of a crude gray ware with broad red lines, were found. The predominant types were a plain buff or brown ware and a polished red ware such as were found at the SU site. A few of the former fall in the category of textured pottery. This is pottery which has been embellished through techniques, such as scoring, incising, or punching, which change the character of the surface. There are no corrugated types in the early Mogollon, but a few pieces have banded necks, or have been scored. Textured pottery became increasingly common in later periods.

Metates were made of unshaped stone blocks and were basin-shaped. Projectile points were short and broad stemmed. Large stemmed blades and stemmed drills were also made. Pipes were made of clay. They were short and were formed in one piece.

Little is known of the physical type of the people and their burial customs, since only one grave has been found which may be attributed to this period. This contained the skeleton of an adult male with a slightly deformed skull who had been buried beneath the floor of a Georgetown house at Starkweather Ruin.

THE SAN FRANCISCO PHASE

Following the Georgetown in New Mexico comes the *San Francisco* stage for which the dates 700 to 900 A. D. have been tentatively suggested.[50] A few datable logs have been found in structures assigned to the latter part of the period. The approximate age is given in round numbers with the terminal date as 900, although two logs gave dates of 927. The terminal date for the Georgetown and the beginning date for the San Francisco stage are by no means firmly established.

There are such distinct changes between Georgetown and San Francisco times, particularly as regards architecture, that an intervening period has been postulated. Excavations in Arizona are thought to provide evidence to substantiate this belief, but there are as yet no published accounts. It has also been suggested that the marked changes were due to outside influences, possibly both Anasazi and Hohokam. Still another theory advanced to account for the architectural changes at the beginning of the San Francisco stage is that the culture was modified by the addition of a Colonial Hohokam house type.[99] It is generally agreed that after about 700 or 800 A. D. the Mogollon was a highly mixed culture, but there are many questions which cannot be answered until more evidence is available. Whatever the explanation,

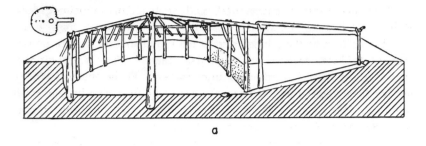

a

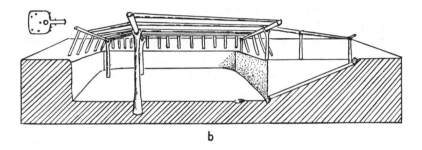

b

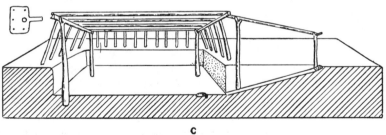

c

Fig. 55—Postulated reconstructions of the dwelling units of the three
Mogollon phases represented by the houses in the Harris Village.
a. Georgetown, b. San Francisco, c. Three Circle.
(After Haury.[50] Courtesy Gila Pueblo.)

many culture traits, notably house types, did change.

The small, roughly circular houses were replaced by deep rectangular pit houses with roofs supported by a main center pole and auxiliary poles along the long axis. Most had side entrances, but in some cases the entrance was through the roof. Some of the wood taken from these houses has yielded tree-ring dates. At Mogollon Village four houses, believed to have been occupied at the close of the period, contained datable logs. The dates fell between 896 and 908 A. D. At

Starkweather Ruin, a house attributed to the San Francisco phase yielded two logs with dates of 927 A. D.

In addition to the domiciliary structures, there were larger houses thought to have been of a ceremonial nature. These were kidney-shaped as a result of the drawing in of the sides at the entrance. They did not have ventilators. Storage pits were rare in houses but occurred frequently between the structures. They were usually undercut, so that they were wider at the bottom than at the top.

The same pottery types found in the Georgetown phase continued to be made and red-on-brown and red-on-white painted wares were also produced. Textured pottery increased in importance and included banded, punched, and scored forms.

Basin-shaped metates persisted, but there were also troughed forms, closed at one end. Grooved mauls are found in San Francisco levels. Grooved axes are not found in all sites, but some were obtained from the San Francisco horizon at Starkweather Ruin. Other stone work included broad-bladed hoes, roughly shaped stone vessels and both long and short pipes. Projectile points, blades, and drills were like the earlier types. A distinctive implement, and an important feature of the Mogollon culture, was a form of bone awl with a notch cut a short distance below the head. Shell work was rare, but a few beads and bracelets made of this material have been found.

Graves are usually found scattered between the structures, although at Starkweather Ruin two adult burials were found below a house floor. Offerings were scarce, but in some cases vessels were broken and the pieces scattered in the grave. This foreshadows the practice of "ceremonial killing" of pottery which became so marked later. It is believed that this was done to permit the release of the spirit or soul of the pottery. While inhumation was the chief method of disposing of the dead, cremation was practiced in a very few cases and the ashes and unconsumed bones placed in pits. This trait may have been derived from the Hohokam to the west. A study of the skeletal remains indicate that the people had relatively low, broad heads and did not practice deformation.

BEAR RUIN [53]

In the seventh and eighth centuries another site of great interest was occupied in east-central Arizona. This site, which is known as the Bear Ruin, lies in the Forestdale Valley some eight miles south of Showlow. Tree-ring dates were obtained from three beams. The dates fall in the middle of the seventh century. These logs may have been cut at any time during the building period, however, and it is only through finding pottery of known age that archaeologists have arrived at the dates of 600 to 800 A. D. for the estimated age of occupation.

Bear Ruin is important because it shows hybridizing and blending of Mogollon and Anasazi traits. Probably the Mogollon was the original culture on which were superimposed certain Anasazi traits. Eventually the former is thought to have been so completely overlaid by the latter as to practically disappear, not only here, but also in other parts of the territory.

The people who lived in Bear Ruin, in the days when it was not a ruin but an inhabited village, were equally dependent on hunting and agriculture. They lived both in round and rectangular pit houses. Seventeen of these have been excavated, and it is thought that this may represent about fifty per cent of the village.

Most of the houses resemble those of the Anasazi area, yet some are like Mogollon houses and others show a combination of Anasazi and Mogollon elements. None contained either masonry or slab linings. A large kiva was found on the outskirts of the village. It contained a grooved trench, dug into the floor, which, it is thought, may have provided a fastening for the lower beams of looms.

Cooking was apparently done over large rock hearths in and about the houses. The technique employed may have been to fill pits with rocks which were then heated. Food wrapped in some insulating material, such as grass, was then placed in the pit and covered with hot rocks topped with earth. This trait is one of those which, it has been suggested, may have been derived from the ancient Cochise people.

The Bear Ruin people did not make any painted pottery, but this must have been a matter of choice, for they were familiar with the painted wares of the Anasazi, Mogollon, and Hohokam, which they imported. A great percentage of the indigenous pottery was the plain buff to reddish-brown ware so plentiful in all early Mogollon sites. One distinctive type of pottery found in the Forestdale Valley is characterized by a black interior and a brown or reddish-brown exterior marked by black fire clouds. These clouds or smudges are the result of pottery coming in contact with fuel during the firing process. Another Forestdale type is a gray to light-brown ware which may represent a fusion of Basketmaker gray ware and Mogollon buff ware. A third is a red-brown pottery mottled by fire clouds.

The dead were buried in shallow pits scattered throughout the village. Bodies usually lay on the back in a semi-flexed position with the heads to the northeast. Most of the graves contained mortuary offerings, usually pottery. One child was found buried with seventeen vessels. Nine of these were miniatures and were possibly his toys. Due to soil conditions, bones were poorly preserved. What evidence could be obtained from them indicates the presence of a mixed population, such as would be expected on the basis of the mixture of traits shown in the material culture.

THE THREE CIRCLE PHASE

In New Mexico further changes took place during the *Three Circle* stage which followed the San Francisco. Pit houses were somewhat smaller and shallower and were all rectangular and often stone-lined. Roofs were usually supported by four main posts placed near the corners. Sometimes the supports were incorporated in the wall. In some cases, the side entrances were short and sometimes started with a step. Besides the domestic structures, there were also larger rectangular pit houses with long inclined entrances which are thought to have been of a ceremonial nature.

Troughed metates entirely replaced the basin-shaped variety. Manos were shaped and four-sided in form. Axes were sometimes notched and sometimes grooved for hafting. Stone vessels were still simple, but were sometimes ornamented with incised patterns. Serrations on both edges characterized the arrow points which were long and narrow-stemmed. Stone palettes appear in this horizon. They may have been inspired or introduced by the Hohokam, or they may have evolved from the simple paint grinding stones such as those found in the SU site. Stone pipes and short clay pipes with fitted stems have been found.

With the exception of red-on-brown pottery, wares already described continued to be made. A black-on-white pottery, which apparently shows a Pueblo influence from the north, was added to the assemblage. Textured pottery became more important.

Shell was widely used as a material, although only a few species were represented. Olivella shells and double-lobed pieces of cut shell were used as beads. Thin bracelets were made of glycymeris shell. Some beads were tubular forms made of bone. Others were made from hackberry seeds, and one infant was found buried with hundreds of these.

In general, burials were like those of the preceding period. Cremations continued to be very rare.

THE MIMBRES PHASE

More and more the Mogollon people were affected by outside cultural influences. By about 950 or 1000 A. D. their culture had been so greatly altered and was submerged to such an extent that the resulting blend may be considered a new entity and given another name. This phase or culture is called the *Mimbres*. It was named after the Mimbres River, for this valley seems to represent the focal point of the culture. The greatest development centers in Grant County, New Mexico, where excavated sites include the Swarts Ruin,[21] the Mattocks Ruin, [98] the Galaz Ruin,[8] and Cameron Creek Village.[6]

In these sites is found evidence of rapid changes in the construction of dwellings. The earliest houses were Mogollon-type pit houses, sometimes slab-lined. These were followed by semi-subterranean and single surface houses with rubble masonry. In the latest stage, houses were built entirely above the surface. They were one-story pueblolike buildings consisting of clusters of rooms. In some cases there were no more than five rooms, in others there were more than fifty. The larger structures sometimes had inner courts or plazas and at Swarts Ruin, where there are two big houses, there was a large dance plaza between the two buildings. Walls were built of masonry, often made of river boulders. Roofs were made of beams covered with brush, grass, reeds, and adobe. Some contained trap-doors, covered with stone slabs, which provided a means of entrance. In one architecturally advanced building there were windows. In the rooms were fireplaces and rock-walled storage bins. Kivas were rectangular, underground chambers.

One interesting trait of the Mimbreños was the practice of burying the dead under the house floors, although the houses continued to be occupied. In one room a total of thirty-two, sub-floor burials were found. Although this practice was the most common one, it was not always followed, for there were some burials outside of the houses and in the fill of unoccupied rooms, and a few cremations have been found.

Archaeologists are very grateful to the ancient Mimbres people for their habit of burying pots with the dead, for it is to this that we owe our knowledge of some of the most beautiful and interesting pottery that has ever been made. A few old people and children were buried without offerings, but most bodies had one or more bowls placed over the head. Metates and manos were also often placed in women's graves, and there was some jewelry. One interesting feature of burial pottery, apart from the magnificent skill which went into its decoration, was the presence of a hole, usually punched into the pot with a sharp instrument, or sometimes drilled. It is believed that this was done to release the spirit or soul of the vessel which was thought to be a part of the maker. The ceremonial killing of pottery probably took place at the grave, for the piece knocked out of a pot is often found associated with it in the burial. Metates were often similarly treated.

The plain burnished-buff and polished-red wares of the Mogollon continued to be made, but black-on-white pottery assumed the greatest importance, and fine corrugated cooking ware began to be produced. There is also some polychrome ware with red and black designs on a white background. It was in the field of black-on-white ware that the ancient Mimbreños reached an artistic peak which has seldom, if ever, been surpassed in the medium of pottery. The black-on-white color combination at once suggests Pueblo influence. Certain design elements are reminiscent of the Hohokam, however.

Bowls were the usual shape. Designs were sometimes positive, sometimes negative. They were of two types, geometric and naturalistic. Both are equally remarkable. The geometric designs are very beautiful and are characterized by an extraordinary sureness of touch which is revealed by the accuracy of spacing and the precision of line. In one case, for example, twenty-seven parallel lines are to be found in a band less than two inches in width. The bowls with naturalistic designs show the same fine sense of composition. Some depict charming, surrealist creatures which Dali might be proud to claim, but others are quite realistic. The forms shown include birds, insects, quadrupeds, fish, and human beings.

From these we can gather certain clues to help us reconstruct something of the way of life of the people who painted them. Turkeys were among the birds most commonly represented, but a lack of turkey bones in the refuse heaps suggests that they were not used for food. Remains of fish, which are also commonly represented, have not been found, but this may, of course, be due to the fragility of their bones. Most useful are the designs showing human beings. There are some narrative scenes which show such activities as men fighting bears, setting snares, dancing, and picking bugs from corn plants. From pictures of people, we may learn something of the clothing which was

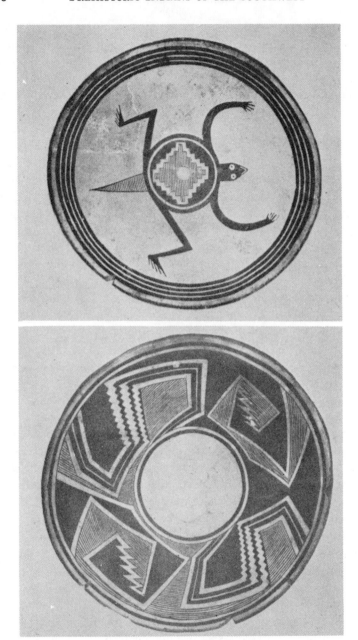

Fig. 56—Mimbres black-on-white pottery. Note hole in center of upper bowl which shows that the vessel has been "killed." (Courtesy School of American Research.)

worn. Men are shown wearing breech cloths. Women are sometimes represented wearing a fringed sash and sandals. Some are shown .wearing blankets which extend below the waist and with fringed sashes hanging down in back. Their hair was worn in whorls on the side, much like the present head dress of unmarried Hopi girls. We know from burials that skull deformation was widely practiced, and this adds to our knowledge of the appearance of the people. Jewelry was rather widely worn. It is shown on human figures painted on bowls, and examples are found in graves. Beads were made of stone and shell. Turquoise was used in the manufacture of beads, in inlaying, and in making pendants which were worn as ear bobs. There were many bracelets and carved pendants of shell.

Stone implements include grooved axes, hoes, large knives, projectile points, and manos and troughed metates. Some interesting artifacts are mortars and pestles believed to have been used for crushing nuts and seeds. Some mortars were holes dug into rock outcrops and boulders. A considerable number of palettes have been found. Bone was widely used in the manufacture of awls. Some of these have decorated heads carved in the form of mountain sheep.

During the twelfth century the Mimbres people left their old haunts. The culture may have persisted for some time in some of the outlying districts to the south but the main area was left unoccupied. During Regressive-Pueblo times it was inhabited for a time by Pueblo people, but there were no occupied villages at the time of Coronado. Why the Mimbreños deserted this fertile valley, we do not know. There is no evidence of warfare and no sign of a hurried departure. When the people moved they must have had time to gather their belongings together and take them with them, for only heavy stone artifacts were left behind. We do not know where these people went after leaving the Mimbres Valley. The best guess seems to be that they moved south into Mexico where they were assimilated and absorbed by other groups, and that they lost their identity among the people of Chihuahua.

SUMMARY

We may summarize the Mogollon problem as follows: In west-central New Mexico and east-central Arizona have been found certain sites which do not follow entirely the same pattern as Anasazi or Hohokam sites. There are a number of possible theories to explain the development of the culture represented by these sites. It may have been derived from the Anasazi, it may represent an early fusion of the Anasazi and Hohokam cultures or, it may be a separate cultural entity which possibly developed from the eastern branch of the ancient Cochise Culture. During the earliest periods it had certain traits which, in the opinion of many archaeologists, make it necessary to consider it a separate basic culture. Houses were of the pit house type with long sloping entrances. Agriculture was practiced, but there was a great dependence on the gathering of wild foods and on hunting. The atlatl was used, as well as the bow. Pottery was made by a coiling and scraping technique, was fired in an oxiding atmosphere, and was usually well polished. A painted ware with red designs on a brown background and a red-on-white ware were later added and textured pottery increased in importance. Pipes were made of clay and of stone. Bone awls were often notched on one side. The dead were usually buried outside the houses. There were some cremations.

From about 700 or 800 A. D. on, there is evidence of more and more outside influences. By around 950 or 1000 A. D. there were so many changes in the Mimbres Valley that the resulting blend is often referred to as a separate culture. Single pit houses were replaced by multi-roomed pueblolike structures built above the ground. Black-on-white pottery was the dominant ware and reached a high degree of excellence. The dead were usually buried under house floors. Cranial deformation was widely practiced. The Mimbres Valley was deserted in the middle of the twelfth century and we can only conjecture where the people who had inhabited it went.

As may readily be seen, the whole Mogollon problem appears to be very complex. This is always the case when a culture or an area is first investigated and the long job of studying it is in its initial stages. Apparently the Mogollon people influenced their neighbors to the north and to the west, and were influenced by them, but we are not yet in a position to evaluate these trends.

CHAPTER VI

THE SINAGUA PEOPLE [18]

In northern Arizona have been found many remains of prehistoric people who were contemporaneous with and had certain traits in common with the Anasazi, and it was originally thought that they all belonged to this culture. Later, and more intensive, studies have shown that the problem is more complex than was first believed. Apparently various tribes were represented, and at present archaeologists are not in agreement as to the cultures to which all of these groups should be assigned.[29] The people of the Kayenta region were Anasazis, but in north-central and northwestern parts of the state lived other people whose affiliations are not yet known with certainty. It has been suggested that the best known group may represent a branch of the Mogollon but it has not been definitely assigned to this culture.

This group is called the *Sinagua*. It first occupied the area about the San Francisco Mountains and, later, the Verde Valley. The characteristic pottery is a brown utility ware of paddle-and-anvil manufacture, fired in an oxidizing atmosphere. The surface is smoothed and sometimes polished. Tree-ring dates have not been satisfactorily established for the earliest period, but, on the basis of pottery finds, it has been estimated that the San Francisco Mountain area was occupied between 500 and 700 A. D. by people who lived in round and rectangular pit houses with center firepits and long sloping entrances to the east. Roofs were of sloping poles covered with earth.

These were followed by fairly deep, timber pit houses. Walls were made of a series of upright poles lashed together, with larger poles set in corners to provide support for a roof platform. The entire structure was covered with grass or bark, and earth was banked over it. These timber pit houses at first had long sloping entrances to the east, but these were later reduced to serve as ventilators, and entrance was through the roof.

In locations unsuitable for the construction of pit houses, there were also surface or near-surface houses. In places where drainage was poor and the ground was boggy, they were built on artificially constructed earth mounds some eight to twelve inches high. These have been called platform or alcove houses. They are roughly rectangular and have a small extension or alcove which was used as an entrance. The alcove may have served a further purpose and supplied additional storage space, although rectangular surface granaries made of timber seem to be associated with these houses.

Fig. 57—Map of the Southwest showing probable areas occupied by the Sinagua group and the Patayan Culture. Dotted area, Sinagua; 1. Southern branch, 2. Northern branch. Hatched area, Patayan; 3. Cohonina branch, 4. Prescott branch. (Based on maps by Colton[16 18] and McGregor.[87])

Sometime between 1046 and 1070 A. D., probably in 1066, a volcano fifteen miles northeast of the present town of Flagstaff erupted. This volcano, now known as Sunset Crater, covered some 800 square miles with a black ash, and forced the early inhabitants to flee from their homes on the lower slopes of the San Francisco Mountains. This seeming disaster, however, was really a very fortunate occurrence, for the fine black material strewn over the countryside by the volcano provided a mulch which aided in conserving moisture and made the practice of agriculture possible over a wider area.

Not only did the original Sinagua people return to the area, but

Fig. 58—Montezuma Castle National Monument, Arizona.
(Courtesy National Park Service.)

Hohokam and Pueblo people moved in too, bringing with them their own special traits. The Hohokam introduced their type of architecture and their distinctive ball courts, and the Anasazi introduced the Pueblo architecture which was adopted by the Sinaguans. At first, masonry was used to replace timbers in pit houses, but in a very short time the Sinagua people began building surface masonry dwellings and multi-roomed pueblos became the rule.

During the years of the great drought of 1276 to 1299, many more people left the area and moved farther south into the Hohokam territory where some Sinaguans had already settled. Shortly after 1300 A. D. the Flagstaff area was abandoned. Some people stayed in the Verde Valley and built large pueblos. This southern branch is best known from the impressive sites of Tuzigoot [13] and Montezuma Castle, now National Monuments. Others may have gone farther south and mixed with the Hohokam in the Gila Basin, and some may have moved to the Little Colorado area and may be among the ancestors of the present Hopi Indians.

CHAPTER VII

THE PATAYAN CULTURE

The prehistoric people who lived in the valley of the Colorado River below the Grand Canyon are the least well known in the Southwest, for most information about them has been derived only from surface surveys. Originally, the term *Yuman* was applied to these people, for Indians speaking a Yuman language were found there by the first white men to visit the area.[35] Some archaeologists still use this term, and it is commonly applied to the culture found in the lower Colorado River basin and adjacent areas in California.[116] Others feel that it is unwise to apply a linguistic term to a prehistoric culture and use the term *Patayan,* a Walapai word meaning "the old people."[16] It is postulated that the Patayan or Yuman is a basic culture or root to which should be given the same status as the Anasazi and Hohokam.

A large population was found in this area when it was visited by Father Kino in 1700, and it is thought that there must have been a great concentration of population in this fertile valley and delta for a long time. In the lower basin of the Colorado River and in the desert area which adjoins it, has been found evidence of ancient people who worked in stone but did not make pottery.[115] A period followed in which more territory was occupied and in which pottery was made. The finding of datable pieces of trade wares in the valley indicates a period of occupation of some 1500 years by people familiar with ceramics.[116]

Archaeologists studying the Patayan or Yuman culture encounter many difficulties. The culture seems to be characterized by a great poverty of material remains, possibly because of a greater use of perishable materials which have not been preserved. Also, until Boulder Dam was built, the river overflowed its banks every year and covered the land with a layer of silt, thus burying much evidence of occupation.[17]

In western and northwestern Arizona, the portion of this area which lies within the scope of this book, the one group of people which has been more or less definitely assigned to the Patayan culture is known only from the finding of distinctive, brown utility-wares. The main center of this tribe seems to have been in the Colorado River valley below Black Canyon.

There are also two other groups of northwestern Arizona which may, or may not, prove to be manifestations of the Patayan pattern.

The area below the Grand Canyon and north of the San Francisco Mountains, bounded on the east by the Little Colorado River and on the west by the Grand Wash Cliffs, was occupied between about 700 and 1100 A. D. by a group of people to which the name *Cohonina* has been applied.[16] These people lived both in deep and in very shallow pit houses with walls made of timber. It has been suggested that the deep pit houses may represent a Sinagua trait and that the near-surface houses were the true Cohonina form. Masonry was used in the construction of some of the deep pit houses and granaries and forts. The latter are large rectangular buildings with thick walls and parapets which were probably loop-holed. The building of such structures would suggest unsettled conditions. Some time after 1100 A. D., masonry pueblos were built.

Cohonina pottery was a gray ware made by the paddle-and-anvil process, sometimes scraped for final finishing, and fired in a reducing atmosphere. Red paint was often applied over the surface of the vessel after firing. It is impermanent and is commonly called "'fugitive red". Occasionally crude designs were applied with a thin black paint. Jars were the most common form, but some bowls were also made. Arrowheads were of a distinctive type. Cohonina points are slender and roughly triangular, although sometimes the maximum breadth is above the base. They are serrated and unnotched. Little is known of methods of disposing of the dead. It is suspected that cremation was practiced, but that the bones were not gathered after burning.

To the south in the vicinity of Prescott, Arizona, between about 900 and 1000 A. D., lived another group of people.[16] They too built some masonry forts and made gray, paddle-and-anvil pottery with a coarse temper containing much mica. Decorations were in black paint. The firing atmosphere was poorly controlled, and there is a variation in color from gray to orange or red, although the paste is the same.

If all this seems needlessly confusing, it must be remembered that even the archaeologists most intimately concerned with the problem are confused too. Only the most fragmentary evidence has been found, but they know that an important chapter in the prehistory of the Southwest lies in the valley of the Colorado River and adjacent areas. They know that eventually they will be able to read it, and, as a result, they will have a greatly improved perspective in their attempts to analyze the whole of prehistoric life in the Southwest. Before the final pages are deciphered, however, so much remains to be done that very likely there will be even more confusion before there is clarification.

CONCLUSION

In the preceding chapters an attempt has been made to summarize our present knowledge of the prehistory of the great area called the Southwest. Although the Southwest is possibly the best known area in America, we have barely scratched the surface and great discoveries lie ahead. For the present there are many gaps in our knowledge. Doubtless in many cases, data have been incorrectly interpreted. Archaeological opinions are by no means unanimous on all points. In the years to come, other archaeologists with greater knowledge and more refined techniques will reveal new pages of prehistory and reinterpret many of those which their predecessors have tried to decipher. The findings of all science must be regarded, "not as rigid dogma, but as reasonable approximation to truth, certain to be largely extended and modified in the future."* Although there is yet much to be learned and much to be reevaluated, a great deal has already been accomplished in the realm of Southwestern archaeology. Through scattered clues, carefully assembled and painstakingly studied and correlated it is at least possible to see something of the growth and development of unfamiliar cultures.

Inevitably certain questions are asked of those who devote themselves to such work. "What good is archaeology?" "Why is it important to know these things?" The best answer seems to be still another question. "Are we sufficiently sure of the worth of our own achievements to deny the value of trying to reconstruct another chapter of human history, even if we have nothing more than pottery and stone to guide us?"** According to our standards the prehistoric inhabitants of the Southwest did not achieve civilization. Still, there might be something to be learned from people so uncivilized that they believed that the cultivation of the land, the creation of beautiful as well as useful objects, and keeping in harmony with the great natural forces of the universe, were more important than the subjugation or destruction of their fellow men.

---

* Ref. 14 p.281
**Ref. 31 p.269

GLOSSARY

Aborigine—The native inhabitants of a country; in America, the Indians.

Apocynum—A plant, related to the milkweed, which provided fibers used in weaving.

Archaeology—The scientific study of the material remains of human life and human activities in prehistoric or ancient times.

Artifact—A product of human workmanship. Commonly used by archaeologists in speaking of prehistoric tools, implements, etc.

Atlatl—An Aztec word meaning spear-thrower. Atlatls are throwing sticks which have a handle on one end and on the other a spur which fits into a pit or cup drilled into the basal end of a dart shaft. When the dart is thrown the atlatl remains in the hand.

Basic Culture—See *Culture*.

Caliche—A crust or succession of crusts of calcium carbonate that forms within or on top of the soil of arid or semi-arid regions.

Ceramic—Pertaining to pottery and its materials.

Chronology—The study of the method of arranging past events or the material representing them in a sequence of their happenings in relation to years or in relation to each other.

Cist—An oval or circular pit, often slab-lined, used for storage. Cists sometimes served a secondary purpose as depositories for the dead.

Clan—A social group made up of a number of households, the heads of which claim descent in either the male or female line from a common ancestor.

Cloisonne—A surface decoration produced by outlining a design with strips of flat wire and filling the interstices with enamel.

Complex—A group of related traits or characteristics which combine to form a complete activity, process, or cultural unit.

Compound—In the Orient, a wall or fenced enclosure containing a house, buildings, etc. The term is also used to describe the walled enclosures built during Classic Hohokam times.

Corrugated Pottery—Pottery in which the alternate ridges and depressions resulting from a coiling-and-pinching technique of manufacture have not been obliterated.

Coursed Masonry—Masonry contructed of stones lying on approximately level beds.

Cranium—Skull (Plural: Crania)

Culture—The total activities and beliefs of a group of individuals which may be separated from other groups on the basis of differences in complexes and original differences in geographical and chronological positions. In an achaeological context, the material remains of a group of people which represent traits which they had in common, which differentiated them from other people. A *Basic Culture* is, as the name implies, one which provides a base or foundation for succeeding cultures. It is essentially a cultural root from which may spring stems and branches.

Deflector—An upright slab, standing between fireplace and ventilator in a pit house or kiva, designed to protect the fire from inrushing air.

Dendrochronology—A system of establishing an absolute count of years by utilizing the pattern combinations of tree-rings.

Diffusion—The transference of elements of--culture from one society to another.

Effigy—An image of a living object.

Ethnology—The scientific study of the cultures of living primitive peoples.

Hatchures—Short, closely spaced, parallel lines used in pottery designs.

Hogan—A Navajo house; one room, domed or conically shaped, made of logs, sometimes with stone side walls, usually covered with earth.

Horizon—In a site, a level or stratum. In a culture, a particular level of development.

Incised—In pottery, grooved in soft clay with a sharp tool.

Jacal—A type of construction in which walls are made of upright poles set at short intervals and heavily plastered with adobe.

Katchinas—Supernatural beings in Pueblo Indian mythology, or masked dancers personifying these beings.

Killed Pottery—Pottery in which a hole has been punched or drilled in order to release the soul or spirit of the vessel which is conceived as being a part of the maker.

Kiva—A ceremonial chamber, usually subterranean and circular.

Mano—A hand stone, usually roughly oblong, used for grinding grains, seeds, etc.

Metate—The grinding stone on which the Mano is rubbed.

Moraine—An accumulation of earth, stones, etc. carried and finally deposited by a glacier.

Oxidizing Atmosphere—Pottery is said to have been fired in an oxidizing atmosphere when air is permitted to circulate around it during the firing process. This leads to an excess of oxygen in the atmosphere and produces pottery in shades of red, brown, or yellow.

Paddle-and-Anvil—A pottery-finishing technique in which coil impressions are obliterated by striking the exterior of the vessel with a paddle while holding a round or mushroom-shaped object, known as an anvil, within the vessel to receive the force of the blow.

Periphery—In archaeological usage, a marginal area, a region lying immediately beyond the boundaries of a specific area.

Pilaster—A square column forming part of a wall.

Phase—This term is used in different ways by different archaeologists. For the purposes of this book, it may be defined as an interval of culture occurring in a specific area at a specific time and associated with a particular culture. It may also be defined as a group of sites with similar determinants.

Polychrome Pottery—Pottery bearing three or more colors.

Plaza—A public square.

Projectile Point—An arrow point, spear point, or dart point.

Reducing Atmosphere—Pottery is said to have been fired in a reducing atmosphere when air is not allowed to circulate around it during the firing process. This results in a reduction of the oxygen content of the atmosphere and produces pottery in shades of white and gray.

Sherd—A fragment of a broken, pottery vessel.

Sipapu—A hole commonly found in the floors of kivas which is symbolic of the mythological place from which, according to creation myths, the first people emerged from the underworld.

Slip—A coating of very fine clay applied to a vessel before firing to give a smooth finish.

Spall—A chip or flake removed from a larger piece of stone.

Stockade—An enclosure made with posts and stakes.

Stratification—The characteristic of being in layers or strata and the processes by which such material is deposited. A single layer is called a *Stratum,* more than one, *Strata.* When undisturbed the lowest stratum is the oldest since it was laid down first.

Trait—Any single element of culture.

Temper—Non-plastic material added to clay from which pottery is made to prevent cracking.

Twilling—A system of weaving in which the woof thread is carried over one and under two or more warp threads, producing diagonal lines or ribs on the surface of the fabric or basket.

Twining—A system of weaving in which splints or threads are intertwined around a foundation of radiating rods or threads.

Tuff—Solidified volcanic ash.

Typology—The study of any system of arrangement according to type.

Bibliography

Amsden, Charles A.
(1)   1939. The Ancient Basketmakers: Southwest Museum Leaflet No. 11, Los Angeles, California.

Bartlett, Katharine
(2)   1934. Material Culture of Pueblo II in the San Francisco Mountains: Museum of Northern Arizona Bulletin 7, Flagstaff, Arizona.

Beals, Ralph L., G. W. Brainerd and Watson Smith
(3)   1945. Archaeological Studies in Northeast Arizona: Univ. of Calif. Pub. in Am. Arch. and Ethn. Vol. 44, No. 1, Berkeley, California.

Benedict, Ruth
(4)   1934. Patterns of Culture: Houghton-Mifflin Co., New York.

Boekelman, H. J.
(5)   1936. A Shell Trumpet from Arizona: American Antiquity, Vol. II, No. 1, pp. 27-31, Menasha, Wisconsin.

Bradfield, Wesley
(6)   1929. Cameron Creek Village, a Site in the Mimbres Area in Grant County, New Mexico: School of American Research, Santa Fe, New Mexico.

Brew, John Otis
(7)   1946. Archaeology of Alkali Ridge, Southeastern Utah. Appendices by Alice Brues and Volney H. Jones: Papers of the Peabody Museum of Am. Arch. and Ethn., Harvard University, Vol. XXI, Cambridge, Mass.

Bryan, B.
(8)   1931. Excavation of the Galaz Ruin: The Masterkey, Vol. IV, Nos. 6 and 7, pp. 179-189, 221-226, Southwest Museum, Los Angeles, Calif.

Bryan, Kirk
(9)   1941. Correlation of the Deposits of Sandia Cave, New Mexico, with the Glacial Chronology: Smithsonian Misc. Col., Vol. 99, No. 23, Washington.

(10)   1941. Pre-Columbian Agriculture in the Southwest as Conditioned by Periods of Alluviation: Association of American Geographers, Annals, Vol. 31, No. 4, pp. 219-242.

Bryan, Kirk, and Louis L. Ray
(11)   1940. Geologic Antiquity of the Lindenmeier Site in Colorado: Smithsonian Misc. Col. Vol. 99. No. 2, Washington, D. C.

Carter, George F.
(12)   1945. Plant Geography and Culture History in the American Southwest: Viking Fund Publications in Anthropology, No. 5, New York.

Caywood, Louis R. and Edward H. Spicer
(13)   1935. Tuzigoot, the Excavation and Repair of a Ruin in the Verde Valley near Clarkdale, Arizona: Office of Southwestern Monuments, National Park Service, Coolidge, Arizona (Mimeographed).

Cockerell, T. D. A.,
(14)   1946. The Function of Psychology: Letter to the Editor, Science, Vol. 103, No. 2670, p. 281, Lancaster, Pa.

Colton, Harold S.
(15)   1939. The Reducing and Oxidizing Atmosphere in Prehistoric Southwestern Ceramics: American Antiquity, Vol. IV, No. 3, Menasha, Wisconsin.

(16)   1939. Prehistoric Culture Units and their Relationships in Northern Arizona: Museum of Northern Arizona Bull. 17, Flagstaff, Arizona.

(17)   1945. The Patayan Problem in the Colorado River Valley: Southwestern Journal of Anthropology, Vol. I, No. 1, Univ. of New Mexico Press, Albuquerque, New Mexico.

(18)   1946. The Sinagua: A Summary of the Archaeology of the Region of Flagstaff, Arizona: Museum of Northern Arizona Bulletin 22, Flagstaff, Arizona.

Colton, Harold S. and L. L. Hargrave
(19)   1933. Pueblo II in the San Francisco Mountains, Arizona; Pueblo II Houses of the San Francisco Mountains, Arizona: Museum of Northern Arizona Bulletin 4, Flagstaff, Arizona.
(20)   1937. Handbook of Northern Arizona Pottery Wares: Museum of Northern Arizona, Bulletin 11, Flagstaff, Arizona.

Cosgrove, H. S. and C. B.
(21)   1932. The Swarts Ruin, a typical Mimbres Site in Southwestern New Mexico: Peabody Museum Papers Vol. XV, No. 1, Harvard University, Cambridge, Mass.

Cummings, Byron
(22)   1940. Kinishba. A prehistoric Pueblo of the Great Pueblo Period: Hohokam Museums Association and University of Arizona, Tucson, Arizona.

Douglass, A. E.
(23)   1929. The Secret of the Southwest Solved by the Talkative Tree-rings: National Geographic Magazine, Vol. 54, pp. 737-770, Washington, D. C.

Fewkes, J. W.
(24)   1911. Antiquities of the Mesa Verde National Park; Cliff Palace: Bulletin 51, Bureau of American Ethnology, Washington, D. C.

Figgins, J. D.
(25)   1927. The Antiquity of Man in America: Natural History, Vol. XXVII, No. 3, pp. 229-239, New York.

Gladwin, Harold S.
(26)   1928. Excavations at Casa Grande, Arizona: Southwest Museum Paper No. 2, Los Angeles, California.
(27)   1937. Excavations at Snaketown: Comparisons and Theories: Medallion Papers, No. XXVI, Gila Pueblo, Globe, Arizona.
(28)   1942. Excavations at Snaketown: Revisions: Medallion Papers, No. XXX, Gila Pueblo, Globe, Arizona.
(29)   1943. A Review and Analysis of the Flagstaff Culture: Medallion Papers, No. XXXI, Gila Pueblo, Globe, Arizona.
(30)   1947. Personal Communication.

Gladwin, Harold S.,[a] Emil W. Haury,[b] E. B. Sayles,[c] and Nora Gladwin.[d]
(31)   1937. Excavations at Snaketown: Material Culture: Medallion Papers, No. XXV, Gila Pueblo, Globe, Arizona.

Gladwin, Winifred and Harold S.
(32)   1929. The Red-on-Buff-Culture of the Gila Basin: Medallion Papers No. II, Gila Pueblo, Globe, Arizona.
(33)   1930. Some Southwestern Pottery Types, Series I: Medallion Papers No. VIII, Gila Pueblo, Globe, Arizona.
(34)   1933. Some Southwestern Pottery Types, Series III: Medallion Papers No. XIII, Gila Pueblo, Globe, Arizona.
(35)   1934. A Method for the Designation of Cultures and their Variations: Medallion Papers, No. XIV, Gila Pueblo, Globe, Arizona.
(36)   1935. The Eastern Range of the Red-on-Buff Culture: Medallion Papers XVI, Gila Pueblo, Globe, Arizona.

Guernsey, S. J.
(37)   1931. Explorations in Northeastern Arizona: Peabody Museum Papers, Vol. XII, No. 1, Harvard University, Cambridge, Mass.

Guernsey, S. J. and A. V. Kidder
(38)   1921. Basket-maker Caves of Northeastern Arizona: Peabody Museum Papers, Volume VIII, No. 2, Harvard University, Cambridge, Mass.

Hack, J. T.
(39)   1941. The Changing Physical Environment of the Hopi Indians of Arizona: Peabody Museum Papers, Vol. XXXV, No. 1, Harvard University, Cambridge, Mass.

Hall, Edward Twitchell, Jr.
(40)   1944. Recent Clues to Athapaskan Prehistory in the Southwest: American Anthropologist, Vol. 46, No. 1, pp. 98-105, Menasha, Wis.
(41)   1944. Early Stockaded Settlements in the Governador, New Mexico. A Marginal Anasazi Development from Basket Maker III to Pueblo I Times; Columbia University Press, New York.

Hargrave, Lyndon L.
(42)   1930. Prehistoric Earth Lodges of the San Francisco Mountains: Museum Notes, Vol. III, No. 5, Museum of Northern Arizona, Flagstaff, Arizona.
(43)   1932. Guide to Forty Pottery Types from the Hopi Country and the San Francisco Mountains, Arizona: Museum of Northern Arizona Bulletin No. 1, Flagstaff, Arizona.

Hargrave, Lyndon L.
(44)   1933. Pueblo II houses of the San Francisco Mountains, Arizona: Museum of Northern Arizona Bulletin 4, pp. 15-75, Flagstaff, Arizona.

Harrington, Mark Raymond
(45)   1924. The Ozark Bluff-Dwellers: American Anthropologist, N. S. Vol. XXVI, No. 1, Menasha, Wisconsin.
(46)   1927. A Primitive Pueblo City in Nevada: American Anthropologist, N. S. Vol. XXIX, No. 3, pp. 262-277, Menasha, Wisconsin.
(47)   1933. Gypsum Cave, Nevada: Southwest Museum Papers, No. 8, Los Angeles, California.

Haury, Emil W.
(48)   1932. Roosevelt 9:6, a Hohokam Site of the Colonial Period: Medallion Papers, No. XI, Gila Pueblo, Globe, Arizona.
(49)   1935. Tree-Rings—The Archaeologist's Time Piece: American Antiquity, Vol. I, No. 2, Menasha, Wisconsin.
(50)   1936. The Mogollon Culture of Southwestern New Mexico: Medallion Papers, No. XX, Gila Pueblo, Globe, Arizona.
(51)   1936. Some Southwestern Pottery Types, Series IV: Medallion Papers, No. XIX, Gila Pueblo, Globe, Arizona.
(52)   1937. A Pre-Spanish Rubber Ball from Arizona: American Antiquity, Vol. II, No. 4, Menasha, Wisconsin.
(53)   1940. Excavations in the Forestdale Valley, East-Central Arizona: University of Arizona Social Science Bulletin No. 12, Tucson, Arizona.
(54)   1943. A Possible Cochise-Mogollon-Hohokam Sequence: Recent Advances in American Archaeology, Proceedings of the American Philosophical Society, Vol. 86, No. 2, Philadelphia, Pennsylvania.
(55)   1943. The stratigraphy of Ventana Cave, Arizona: American Antiquity, Vol. VIII, No. 3, Menasha, Wisconsin.
(56)   1945. The Excavation of Los Muertos and Neighboring Ruins in the Salt River Valley, southern Arizona: Peabody Museum Papers, Vol. XXIV, No. 1, Harvard University, Cambridge, Massachusetts.
(57)   1945. Arizona's Ancient Irrigation Builders: Natural History, Vol. LIV, No. 7, New York.
(58)   1946. Report on Field Work in Notes and News: American Antiquity, Vol. XII, No. 1, Menasha, Wisconsin.
(59)   1947. Personal Communication.

Hawley, Florence M.
         1936. Field Manual of Prehistoric Southwestern Pottery Types: University of New Mexico Anthropological Series, Bulletin 291, Vol. I, No. 4, Albuquerque, New Mexico.

Hendron, J. W.
(60)   1940. Prehistory of El Rito de los Frijoles, Bandelier National Monument: Southwestern Monuments Association, Technical Series, No. 1, Coolidge, Arizona.

Hewett, Edgar L.
(61)   1935. The Chaco Canyon and its Monuments: Handbooks of Archaeological History, University of New Mexico and School of American Research, Albuquerque, New Mexico.

Hewett, Edgar L.
(62)   1938. The Pajarito Plateau and its Ancient People: Handbooks of Archaeological History, University of New Mexico and School of American
Research, Albuquerque, New Mexico.

Hibben, Frank C.
(63)   1938. The Gallina Phase: American Antiquity, Vol. IV, No. 2, pp. 131-136,
Menasha, Wisconsin.
(64)   1941. Evidences of Early Occupation in Sandia Cave, New Mexico, and
other sites in the Sandia-Manzano Region: Smithsonian Miscellaneous Collections, Vol. 99, No. 23.

Howard, Edgar B.
(65)   1935. Evidence of Early Man in North America: The Museum Journal,
Vol. XXIV, Nos. 2-3, University of Pennsylvania, Philadelphia,
Pennsylvania.

Hurst, C. T.
(66)   1945. Completion of Excavation of Tabequache Cave II: Southwestern
Lore, Vol. II, No. 1, Gunnison, Colorado.
(67)   1946. Colorado's Old Timers: Colorado Archaeological Society, Gunnison,
Colorado.

Huscher, Betty H. and Harold A.
(68)   1943. The Hogan Builders of Colorado: Colorado Archaeological Society,
Gunnison, Colorado.

Jenks, Albert E.
(69)   1936. Pleistocene Man In Minnesota, a Fossil *Homo Sapiens*: Minneapolis,
Minnesota.
(70)   1937. Minnesota's Browns Valley Man and Associated Burial Artifacts:
Memoirs, American Anthropological Association, No. 49, Menasha,
Wisconsin.

Judd, Neil M.
(71)   1925. Everyday Life in Pueblo Bonito: National Geographic Magazine, Vol.
XLVIII, No. 3, pp. 227-262, Washington, D. C.
(72)   1940. Progress in the Southwest: Smithsonian Miscellaneous Collections,
Volume 100, Washington, D. C.

Kidder, Alfred Vincent
(73)   1924. An Introduction to the Study of Southwestern Archaeology, with a
Preliminary Account of the Excavations at Pecos: Papers, Southwestern Expedition, Phillips Acadamy, No. 1, Yale University Press,
New Haven, Conn.
(74)   1927. Southwestern Archaeological Conference: Science, Vol. 66, No. 1716,
pp. 489-91, Lancaster, Pennsylvania.
(75)   1931. The Pottery of Pecos: Vol. I, Papers, Southwestern Expedition,
Phillips Academy, Yale University Press, New Haven, Conn.

Kidder, Alfred Vincent and S. J. Guernsey
(76)   1919. Archaeological Explorations in Northeastern Arizona: Bureau of
American Ethnology, Bulletin No. 65, Washington, D. C.

Kidder, Alfred Vincent and Anna O. Shepard
(77)   1936. The Pottery of Pecos: Vol. II, Papers, Southwestern Expedition,
Phillips Academy, Yale University Press, New Haven, Connecticut.

Kroeber, A. L.
(78)   1928. Native Culture of the Southwest: Univ. of California Pub. in Am.
Arch. and Ethn., Vol. XXIII, No. 9, pp. 373-398, Berkeley, Calif.

Linton, Ralph
(79)   1936. The Study of Man: D. Appleton-Century Co. New York.
(80)   1944. Nomad Raids and Fortified Pueblos: American Antiquity, Vol. X,
No. 1, Menasha, Wisconsin.

Martin, Paul S., Lawrence Roys and Gerhardt von Bonin
(81)   1936. Lowry Ruin in Southwestern Colorado: Anthropological Series, Vol.
XXIII, No. 1, Field Museum of Natural History, Chicago, Illinois.

Martin, Paul S., Carl Lloyd and Alexander Spoehr
(82)   1938. Archæological Field Work in the Ackmen-Lowry Area, Southwestern Colorado, 1937. Anthropological Series, Vol. XXIII, No. 2, Field Museum of Natural History, Chicago, Illinois.
Martin, Paul S. and John Rinaldo
(83)   1939. Modified Basket Maker Sites, Ackmen-Lowry Area, Southwestern Colorado, 1938: Anthropological Series, Vol. XXIII, No. 3, Field Museum of Natural History, Chicago, Illinois.
Martin, Paul S., John Rinaldo, and Marjorie Kelly
(84)   1940. The SU Site, Excavations at a Mogollon Village, Western New Mexico, 1939. Anthropological Series, Vol. XXXII, No. 1, Field Museum of Natural History, Chicago, Illinois.
Martin, Paul S., Robert J. Braidwood, John Rinaldo, Marjorie Kelly and Brigham A. Arnold.
(85)   1943. The SU Site, Excavations at a Mogollon Village, Western New Mexico: Second Season, 1941. Anthropological Series, Vol. 32, No. 2, Field Museum of Natural History, Chicago, Illinois.
McGregor, John C.
(86)   1941. Winona and Ridge Ruin: Part I, Northern Arizona Society of Science and Art, Bulletin 18, Flagstaff, Arizona.
(87)   1941. Southwestern Archaeology: John Wiley & Sons, Inc., New York.
(88)   1943. Burial of an Early American Magician: Recent Advances in American Archaeology, Proceeding of the American Philosophical Society, Vol. 86, No. 2, Philadelphia, Pennsylvania.
Mera, Harry P.
(89)   1934. Observations on the Archaeology of Petrified Forest National Monument: Laboratory of Anthropology, Tech. Bulletin 7, Santa Fe, New Mexico.
(90)   1935. Ceramic Clues to the Prehistory of North Central New Mexico. Tech. Bulletin 8, Santa Fe, New Mexico.
(91)   1938. Some Aspects of the Largo Cultural Phase, Northern New Mexico: American Antiquity, Vol. III, No. 3, Menasha, Wisconsin.
Morris, Earl H.
(92)   1925. Exploring in the Canyon of Death: National Geographic Magazine, Volume XLVIII, No. 3, pp. 262-300, Washington, D. C.
(93)   1927. The Beginnings of Pottery Making in the San Juan Area, Unfired Prototypes and the Wares of the Earliest Ceramic Period: Anthropological Papers, American Museum of Natural History, Vol. XXVIII, Pt. 2, New York.
(94)   1928. The Aztec Ruin: Arch M. Huntington Survey of the Southwest, Anthropological Papers, American Museum of Natural History, Vol. Vol. XXVI, Pts. 1-5. New York.
(95)   1939. Archaeological Studies in the La Plata District, Southwestern Colorado and Northwestern New Mexico: Appendix by Anna O. Shepard. Carnegie Institution, Washington, D. C.
(96)   1946. Personal Communication.
Morss, Noel
(97)   1931. The Ancient Culture of the Fremont River in Utah: Peabody Museum Papers, Vol. XII, No. 3, Harvard University, Cambridge, Massachusetts.
Nesbitt, Paul H.
(98)   1931. The Ancient Mimbrenos, Based on Investigations at the Mattocks Ruin, Mimbres, Valley, New Mexico: Logan Museum Publications, Bull. No. 4, Beloit, Wisconsin.
(99)   1938. Starkweather Ruin: Logan Museum Publications Bull. No. 6, Beloit, Wisconsin.
Nusbaum, J. L.
(100)   1922. A Basket-Maker Cave in Kane County, Utah; with Notes on the Artifacts by A. V. Kidder and S. J. Guernsey: Indian Notes and Monographs, Museum of the American Indian, No. 29, Heye Foundation, New York.

Parsons, Elsie Clews
(101) 1939. Pueblo Indian Religion: University of Chicago Publications in Anth. and Ethn., Chicago, Illinois.

Reed, Erik K.
(102) 1942. Implications of the Mogollon Complex: American Antiquity, Vol. VIII, No. 1, Menasha, Wisconsin.

Rinaldo, John
(103) 1941. Conjectures on the Independent Development of the Mogollon Culture: American Antiquity, Vol. VII, No. 1, Menasha, Wisconsin.

Roberts, Frank H. H., Jr.
(104) 1929. Recent Archeological Developments in the Vicinity of El Paso, Texas: Smithsonian Miscellaneous Collections, Vol. 81, No. 7, Washington, D. C.

(105) 1929. Shabik'eschee Village, A Late Basket Maker Site in the Chaco Canyon, New Mexico, Bulletin 92, Bureau of American Ethnology, Washington, D. C.

(106) 1930. Early Pueblo Ruins in the Piedra District, southwestern Colorado: Bulletin 96, Bureau of American Ethnology, Washington, D. C.

(107) 1931. The Ruins at Kiatuthlanna, eastern Arizona: Bulletin 100, Bureau of American Ethnology, Washington, D. C.

(108) 1932. The Village of the Great Kivas on the Zuni Reservation, New Mexico, Bulletin 111, Bureau of American Ethnology, Washington, D. C.

(109) 1935. A Folsom Complex. Preliminary Report on Investigations at the Lindenmeier Site in northern Colorado: Smithsonian Miscellaneous Collections, Vol. 94, Washington, D. C.

(110) 1935. A Survey of Southwestern Archeology: American Anthropologist, Vol. XXXVII, No. 1, pp. 1-33, Menasha, Wisconsin.

(111) 1937. Archaeology in the Southwest: American Antiquity, Vol. III, No. 1, pp. 3-33, Menasha, Wisconsin.

(112) 1939. Archeological Remains in the Whitewater District, eastern Arizona; Part I, House Types: Bulletin 121 Bureau of American Ethnology, Washington, D. C.

(113) 1939. The Development of a Unit-Type Dwelling: Hewett Anniversary Volume "So Live The Works of Men", University of New Mexico Press, Albuquerque, New Mexico.

(114) 1942. Archeological and Geological Investigations in the San Jon District, eastern New Mexico: Smithsonian Miscellaneous Collections, Vol. 103, No. 4, Washington, D. C.

Rogers, Malcolm J.
(115) 1939. Early Lithic Industries of the Lower Basin of the Colorado River and Adjacent Desert Areas: San Diego Museum Papers, No. 3, San Diego, California.

(116) 1945. An Outline of Yuman Prehistory: Southwestern Journal of Anthropology, Vol. I, No. 2, pp. 167-198, Albuquerque, New Mexico.

Sayles, E. B.
(117) 1935. An Archaeological Survey of Texas: Medallion Papers, No. XVII, Gila Pueblo, Globe, Arizona.

Sayles, E. B. and Ernst Antevs
(118) 1941. The Cochise Culture: Medallion Papers, No. XXIV, Gila Pueblo, Globe, Arizona.

Seltzer, Carl C.
(119) 1944. Racial Prehistory in the Southwest and the Hawikuh Zunis: Peabody Museum Papers, Vol. XXIII, No. 1, Harvard University, Cambridge, Mass.

Stallings, W. S., Jr.
(120) 1937. Southwestern Dated Ruins: I, Tree-Ring Bulletin, Vol. IV, No. 2, Tucson, Arizona.

(121) 1939. Dating Prehistoric Ruins by Tree-Rings: General Series, Bulletin 8, Laboratory of Anthropology, Santa Fe, New Mexico.

(122) 1941. A Basketmaker II Date from Cave du Pont, Utah: Tree-Ring Bulletin, Vol. VIII, No. 1, Laboratory of Tree-Ring Research, Tucson, Arizona.

Steward, Julian H.
(123) 1933. Archaeological Problems of the Northern Periphery of the Southwest: Bulletin No. 5, Museum of Northern Arizona, Flagstaff, Ariz.

Underhill, Ruth
(124) 1947. First Penthouse Dwellers of America: Second Revised Edition, Laboratory of Anthropology, Santa Fe, N. M.

Watson, Don
(125) 1946. Cliff Palace; the Story of an Ancient City: Mesa Verde National Park Museum, Mesa Verde, Colorado.

Weatherwax, Paul
(126) 1936. The Origin of the Maize Plant and Maize Agriculture in Ancient America: Symposium on Prehistoric Agriculture, Bulletin 296, University of New Mexico, Albuquerque, N. M.

Weltfish, Gene
(127) 1932. Preliminary Classification of Prehistoric Southwestern Basketry: Smithsonian Miscellaneous Collections: Vol. 87, No. 7, Washington, D. C.
(128) 1932. Problems in the Study of Ancient and Modern Basketmakers: American Anthropologist, N. S. Vol. XXXIV, No. 1, pp. 108-117, Menasha, Wisconsin.

Woodward, Arthur
(129) 1931. The Grewe Site: Occasional Papers, No. 1, Los Angeles Museum of History, Science and Art, Los Angeles, California.

Wormington, H. M.
(130) 1944. Ancient Man in North America, (Second Revised Edition): Popular Series, No. 4, Colorado Museum of Natural History, Denver, Colorado.

APPENDIX

Outstanding Exhibit-Sites, Modern Pueblos, Local Museums

by

ERIK K. REED

Regional Archaeologist
National Park Service

After reading about the prehistoric inhabitants of the Southwest many people feel that they would like to visit the places where they lived, examine examples of their ancient arts and crafts, and see their present-day descendents. No description can produce the feeling that one experiences when viewing the imposing ruins found in our National Monuments and Parks. Even a short time spent looking at pottery and other artifacts in a museum will give a far better idea of their appearance than will photographs, drawings, or the most detailed descriptions. A visit to a modern pueblo makes it possible to visualize something of the life of bygone centuries and to think of the ancient inhabitants of the area as living, breathing people rather than as lifeless specimens. The following lists have been prepared in an effort to help those who wish to visit the Southwest and to learn about its people through their own experience.

I. OUTSTANDING EXHIBIT-SITES
The San Juan Anasazi Culture

MESA VERDE NATIONAL PARK.

Great cliff-dwellings and open pueblos of the Classic period. Pithouse, mesa-top villages and cave remains of earlier periods, Modified Basketmaker and Developmental Pueblo. One of the major foci of the Anasazi culture of 300-1300 A. D., and the most accessible and best-exhibited, interpreted by caravan-tours and an outstanding museum. Paved entrance-road from Highway U. S.-160 between Mancos and Cortez, Colorado. Lodge with adequate accommodations open May-October.

CHACO CANYON NATIONAL MONUMENT.

The greatest concentration of open pueblo ruins in a valley floor, another of the major foci of prehistoric Anasazi civilization. The famous huge buildings, Pueblo Bonito, Chetro Ketl, Pueblo del Arroyo, etc.; a restored Great Kiva, an excavated Modified-Basketmaker village; and innumerable small pueblo sites. Undeveloped museum. Very restricted accommodations. In the middle of northwestern New Mexico, 64 miles north of Thoreau (which is on Highway U. S.-66) and 64 miles south of Aztec, New Mexico (on U. S.-550); 25 miles from nearest paved road (State 55, Cuba to Bloomfield).

AZTEC RUINS NATIONAL MONUMENT.

An excavated great pueblo of the Classic period, twelfth and thirteenth centuries, built between 1100 and 1125 A. D., with a completely restored Great Kiva; additional unexcavated pueblo ruins. Lying between Chaco Canyon and the Mesa Verde, these pueblos on the Animas River partake of both phases of Anasazi culture. A small museum adjoining the main ruin. Located close to Highway U. S.-550 and the town of Aztec, New Mexico.

CANYON DE CHELLY NATIONAL MONUMENT.

Striking cliff-dwellings and very early remains. In a spectacular setting of great red-rock canyons occupied by picturesque Navajo Indians. Tree-ring dates from one of the major sites, Mummy Cave, range from 348 A. D.—the earliest date in the San Juan drainage—to 1284 A. D., the next-to-last. No museum. The monument and canyon area extends east of Chinle, Arizona, in the Navajo Indian Reservation. Chinle is 100 miles from Gallup, New Mexico, or seventy-five miles (unpaved) from Chambers, Arizona (which is west of Gallup on Highway U. S.-66). Not accessible in bad weather. An excellent lodge (Thunderbird Ranch, Chinle, Arizona), but rather restricted facilities.

NAVAJO NATIONAL MONUMENT.

Betatakin and Keetseel, great cliff-pueblos of the thirteenth century, picturesquely situated in huge caves in the red sandstone walls of the Tsegi Canyons, west of Kayenta, Arizona, in the Navajo Indian Reservation. No museum. No tourist accommodations. (As in all the other national monuments listed, however, a custodian on duty the year around, resident at headquarters above Betatakin.) Another 100 miles, of rather bad road, from Chinle to Betatakin; or 135 miles from Flagstaff—sixty miles north on paved Highway U. S.-89, about the same distance on fairly good unsurfaced reservation road, and the last dozen miles a quite rough trail. Not accessible in winter or in rainy weather.

The White Mountains Region

KINISHBA.

A large pueblo of the period 1000-1400, largely excavated and partially restored by the Arizona State Museum, in the Apache Indian Reservation near Fort Apache, Arizona, twenty miles east of Highway U. S.-60. No accommodations.

The Rio Grande Area

BANDELIER NATIONAL MONUMENT.

Unusual cliff-ruins and open sites in beautiful Frijoles Canyon, in the Pajarito Plateau, west of Santa Fe and south of Los Alamos, New Mexico, seventeen miles from paved highway. Museum. Small lodge open May-October.

PUYE.

Large partially-restored pueblo and small cliff-ruins, in the Pajarito Plateau, north of Los Alamos, on the Santa Clara Indian Reservation, fifteen miles from Espanola, New Mexico.

CORONADO STATE MONUMENT.

Two extensive adobe pueblos, Kuaua and Puaray, the former partially restored. Museum. Across the Rio Grande from Bernalillo, New Mexico, just off paved Highway State 44.

PECOS STATE MONUMENT.

Ruins of the great pueblo, finally abandoned in 1838, and of the partially-restored Spanish mission of the seventeenth and eighteenth centuries. Close to Highway U.S.-85, about twenty-five miles southeast of Santa Fe, near modern town of Pecos, New Mexico.

GRAN QUIVIRA NATIONAL MONUMENT.

Ruins of the pueblo and mission of Humanas, abandoned about 1675. No museum; no accommodations. By a poor road twenty-five miles south of Mountainair, New Mexico, which is on Highway U. S.-60.

ABO and QUARAI STATE MONUMENTS.

Sister missions to Humanas, with extensive unexcavated pueblo ruins. No museums. Close to U. S.-60 and Mountainair, New Mexico.

The Salado Complex

TONTO NATIONAL MONUMENT.

Two fourteenth century cliff-dwellings high in a small canyon overlooking Roosevelt Lake and the Tonto Basin. These well-preserved ruins have yielded fine and unusual archaeological material: the striking Salado polychrome pottery, a variety of expertly-made cotton textiles, even a lot of lima beans. Very small museum exhibit. No accommodations at the monument. Located near Roosevelt, Arizona, and the Apache Trail (State Highway 88).

CASA GRANDE NATIONAL MONUMENT.

A unique great adobe structure, sole survivor of the large pueblo-like towers and compounds built by the Salado in the Gila Basin in the fourteenth century. The site includes several adobe compounds as well as the Casa Grande itself, and also earlier *Hohokam* remains—unexcavated ball-courts and pit-houses. Small museum. On State Highway 87 close to Coolidge, Arizona.

PUEBLO GRANDE CITY PARK.

A complex mound, partially excavated, of the late period in the Phoenix area. On E. Washington Avenue, Phoenix.

Sinagua Sites

WUPATKI NATIONAL MONUMENT.

Large and small pueblos of 1100-1300 and earlier pit-houses; several Anasazi sites as well as Sinagua—the frontier between these two cultures was not the Little Colorado, but lay some distance west into the Wupatki area, and varied from time to time. Still other cultural influences are observed. One unique feature is a masonry-walled ball-court beside Wupatki Pueblo and near the monument headquarters, fifteen miles east of U. S.-89 and forty-five miles from Flagstaff, Arizona. No museum. No accommodations at the monument.

WALNUT CANYON NATIONAL MONUMENT.

Very small cliff-dwellings in sandstone ledges of a narrow chasm twelve miles east of Flagstaff, not far from Highway 66. No exhibits installed in Museum. No accommodations at the monument.

TUZIGOOT NATIONAL MONUMENT.

An excavated and partially restored hilltop pueblo, which reached its maximum in the fourteenth century. Comparatively large museum housing extensive collection close to Clarkdale, Arizona, and readily accessible from U. S.-89.

MONTEZUMA CASTLE NATIONAL MONUMENT.

A five-story cliff-dwelling of the same period as Tuzigoot pueblo, near Camp Verde, Arizona, and readily accessible from Highway U. S.-89. Small museum. No accommodations at the monument. Also included in this monument is Montezuma Well, nine miles northeast, with small cliff-dwellings in a limestone sinkhole containing a "bottomless" lake. Highly unusual archaeological features at Montezuma Well are cist-graves undercut in soft limestone, and travertine-encrusted prehistoric irrigation ditches.

II. MODERN PUEBLOS ON (AT LEAST APPROXIMATELY) PRE-SPANISH LOCATIONS

ORAIBI on the third or northwesternmost Hopi mesa, materially unchanged for over 600 years, and in a general sense, the other older HOPI INDIAN pueblos—WALPI on First Mesa, SHONGOPOVI and MISHONGNOVI on the middle mesa—which have shifted their locations during the historic period from valley floors to mesa tops. The villages of Hano (Tewa) and Sichomovi on First Mesa, and probably also Shipaulovi on Second Mesa, are eighteenth century foundations. Hotevilla, Bakavi and New Orabi (Kikhochomovi) date from the break-up of Oraibi only about fifty years ago. Toreva and Polacca are purely modern towns. Good dirt roads to the Hopi country from Gallup, Winslow, and Flagstaff. No tourist accommodations.

ZUNI PUEBLO, the one surviving, or reestablished, town of the six early-historic "cities of Cibola." Fair road, forty miles south from Gallup, New Mexico. Very limited tourist accommodations.

ACOMA on its great mesa, one of the most picturesque of all, little changed since the seventeenth century when the large mission church was built. Fair road, thirteen miles south of U. S.-66, about sixty miles west of Albuquerque.

ISLETA, on Highway U. S.-85 about ten miles south of Albuquerque.

The five Keres pueblos southwest of Santa Fe—SANTO DOMINGO, SAN FELIPE, and COCHITI along the Rio Grande north of Bernalillo, west of U. S.-85; ZIA and SANTA ANA on the Jemez River, northwest of Bernalillo and across the stream from State-44.

JEMEZ PUEBLO, twenty-five miles northwest of Bernalillo on State Highway 4.

The five Tewa pueblos north of Santa Fe: TESUQUE, on U. S.-64-285; NAMBE, in the foothills to the northeast; SAN ILDEFONSO, on the east bank of the Rio Grande; SANTA CLARA, on the west bank just below Espanola; SAN JUAN, at Chamita, New Mexico.

TAOS, the one modern terraced pueblo, close to Taos, New Mexico, and PICURIES in the foothills to the south.

In the Rio Grande drainage, Laguna and Sandia are historic pueblos only. Laguna was a new foundation, under Spanish direction, about 1700. Sandia was re-established on or near an earlier location, in 1745-1750 by Tiwa Indians brought back from the Hopi country by Spanish priests, after abandonment fifty years earlier of the several Tiwa pueblos between Bernalillo and Albuquerque.

III. LOCAL ARCHAEOLOGICAL MUSEUMS IN THE SOUTHWEST

Santa Fe: The Laboratory of Anthropology.
            The Museum of New Mexico.

Albuquerque: The University of New Mexico Anthropology Museum.

Tucson: The Arizona State Museum at the University of Arizona.

Phoenix: The Heard Museum.

Grand Canyon National Park: The Wayside Museum of Archaeology.

Petrified Forest National Monument: Small branch museums at Painted Desert Inn and Puerco Ruin.

Flagstaff: The Museum of Northern Arizona

INDEX